Anonymous

Cambridge in the Centennial

Anonymous

Cambridge in the Centennial

ISBN/EAN: 9783337401955

Printed in Europe, USA, Canada, Australia, Japan

Cover: Foto ©ninafisch / pixelio.de

More available books at **www.hansebooks.com**

CAMBRIDGE IN THE "CENTENNIAL."

PROCEEDINGS,

JULY 3, 1875,

IN CELEBRATION OF THE

Centennial Anniversary

OF

WASHINGTON'S TAKING COMMAND

OF THE

CONTINENTAL ARMY,

ON CAMBRIDGE COMMON.

CAMBRIDGE:
PRINTED BY ORDER OF THE CITY COUNCIL.
M DCCC LXXV.

Prepared,

BY ORDER OF THE CITY COUNCIL

AND

COMMITTEE ON THIRD OF JULY CELEBRATION.

BY THE

CLERK OF COMMITTEES.

Cambridge:
Press of John Wilson and Son.

CONTENTS.

	PAGE
CAMBRIDGE COMMON . .	5
WASHINGTON ELM .	7
INTRODUCTORY	9
Acts of Men of Cambridge in 1775 . . .	9
Acts of City of Cambridge in 1875	10
Committee of Arrangements for Celebration, July 3 . .	12
Preliminary Arrangements	13
Invited Guests	14
Form of Invitation	16
THE DECORATIONS	17
THE CELEBRATION	25
Remarks of Mayor Bradford	26
Poem of Prof. James Russell Lowell	27
Address of Andrew P. Peabody, D.D.	39
THE DINNER	63
Remarks of Mayor Bradford	64
Response of Hon. George S. Boutwell	65
,, ,, Governor William Gaston	68
,, ,, Hon. Josiah Quincy	69

CONTENTS.

THE DINNER (*continued*).   PAGE

    Response of Gen. Charles Devens, Jr. 75
    ,,   ,, President Charles W. Eliot 78
    ,,   ,, M. W. Grand Master Percival L. Everett 81
    ,,   ,, Dep't Commander George S. Merrill . . 84
    ,,   ,, Rev. Dr. A. P. Peabody 87
    ,,   ,, Prof. J. Russell Lowell 87
    ,,   ,, Dr. Oliver Wendell Holmes 88
    ,,   ,, Ex.-Gov. Emory Washburn 91
    ,,   ,, Hon. George Washington Warren . . . 95
    ,,   ,, Gen. Edward W. Hincks 96

THE CHILDREN'S ENTERTAINMENT 99
    Members of Chorus and Soloists 100
    Programme 101
    Remarks of Rev. A. B. Muzzey 101
    ,,   ,, James Alexander, Esq. 105
    Poem of Rev. Dr. William Newell 107

THE EVENING CONCERT 113
    Members of Chorus 113
    Programme 113

CITY GOVERNMENT FOR 1875 117

TEACHERS IN THE PUBLIC SCHOOLS 124

CHRONOLOGICAL CATALOGUE 126

STATISTICS 127

CAMBRIDGE IN THE "CENTENNIAL."

"It belongs to us with strong propriety to celebrate this day. The town of Cambridge and the county of Middlesex are filled with the vestiges of the Revolution. Whithersoever we turn our eyes, we behold some accounts of its glorious scenes." — EDWARD EVERETT.

CAMBRIDGE COMMON.

CAMBRIDGE COMMON was granted to the town by the "Proprietors of Common and Undivided Lands in Cambridge" — a private company — on the 20th of November, 1769, by the following vote: —

Voted, That all the common lands belonging to the proprietors, fronting the college (commonly called the Town Commons), not heretofore granted or allotted to any particular person, be, and the same is hereby, granted to the town of Cambridge, to be used as a training-field, to lie undivided, and to remain for that use for ever. Provided, nevertheless, that if the said town shall dispose of, grant, or appropriate the same, or any part thereof, at any time hereafter, to or for any other use than that before mentioned, then, and in such case, the whole of the premises hereby granted to the said town shall revert to the proprietors granting the same; and the present grant shall be deemed null and void, to all intents and purposes, as if the same had never been made."

Besides being the muster-field where the American army of the Revolution had its temporary abiding-place after it was called into being, Cambridge Common is consecrated by other memories. It was the place selected by the settlers of 1630-31 for their intrenched camp. As early as 1632 a tax was levied "for the construction of a palisado about the town for protection against its enemies," and that fortification ran along the northern side of this Common. Here the flag of thirteen stripes was first unfolded to the breeze. Here also, from the greensward, ascended the smoke of a bonfire, into which was contemptuously cast a printed speech of King George the Third, in which that misguided potentate uttered sentiments which were in opposition to the feelings and desires of his "rebellious" subjects, who took that means to express their disgust at the ill-advised and unjust strictures of a weak monarch and his advisers. Here the patriot army, little skilled in the devices of warfare, badly equipped, their ranks thinned by the recent battle at Bunker Hill, were encamped, wanting in almost every thing necessary for soldiers arrayed against a powerful monarchy, except the fervor of patriotic resolve to battle for the right and become victorious, — the fresh remembrances of Concord and Lexington serving to spur them on to future noble deeds. From this camp, too, were despatched guards for Lechmere Point, Prospect Hill, Winter Hill, and various other points; and frequent regimental parades were here held under the supervision of Generals Green, Sullivan, and Heath; and occasionally the whole camp was made glad by the presence of the commander-in-chief, who came from his headquarters near by, on Brattle Street, to mingle with his men, and look after their comfort. The whole number of men at that time encamped in Cambridge was about eight thousand; and their devotion to the cause, and love and respect for their commander, tended to insure them success against unequal odds, and win for us the rights of freemen, which we so proudly cherish.

Near the westerly end of the Common still stands the superb wide-spreading elm under whose shade Washington first drew his sword as general-in-chief of the American army, and known far and wide as

THE WASHINGTON ELM.

Apart from its association with a great event, there is something impressive about this elm. It is a king among trees; a monarch native to the soil, whose subjects, once scattered over the broad plain before it, have all vanished, and left it alone in solitary state.

Tradition says, that, when the surrounding forest was felled by the axe of the woodman, this tree had already attained so great a size that it obtained a respectful immunity from the fate of its neighbors and kin. There it stands to-day, in all its majestic grandeur, one hundred feet in height, its trunk six feet in diameter, and its branches spreading ninety feet, the admiration of each beholder, and daily visited by people from near and distant lands, who look upon it as a place and a thing hallowed by the memories of the past. Though portions of it are somewhat decayed, and the blasts of centuries have passed over it, it is still vigorous; and, if loving care and careful nursing can avail, it will continue to live and flourish for many future generations.

As a shrine of the Revolution, a temple "not made with hands," and the only living witness of the scenes of a hundred years ago, we trust the old elm will long survive, a sacred memorial to those who shall come after us.

INTRODUCTORY.

THE events subsequent to the 5th of March, 1770, when several citizens of the town of Boston were massacred in King (now State) Street by British soldiers, had, by April, 1775, caused Boston to be practically British ground, and a safe abiding-place for Tory refugees; while Cambridge, for the same reasons, was the advanced post of the uprising American Republic, and the temporary abode of many patriots active in the cause.

On the night of April 18th, when British troops, having landed at Lechmere Point, marched thence to Lexington, they were followed by some of the inhabitants of Cambridge, who actively assisted the men of Lexington and Concord in resisting, and forcing a retreat of, their common enemy; and a monument in the ancient burial-ground, opposite the historic buildings of Harvard College, bears the names of —

JOHN HICKS,
WILLIAM MARCY,
MOSES RICHARDSON,
Buried here;

JASON RUSSELL,
JABEZ WYMAN,
JASON WINSHIP,
Buried in Menotomy;

MEN OF CAMBRIDGE
WHO FELL IN DEFENCE OF THE LIBERTY OF THE PEOPLE,
APRIL 19, 1775.

On the evening previous to the battle of Bunker Hill, a regiment of the Provincial troops, under command of

Colonel Prescott, marched from Cambridge Common to its post of duty, after a prayer by the venerable President Langdon, standing upon the step of the building then occupied as the head-quarters of General Ward, and from which General Joseph Warren, after a hasty attempt at repose, doubly called for by the fatiguing duties of the entire night as Chairman of the Committee of Safety and President of the Provincial Congress, went forth to his death. Upon that fatal day, men of Cambridge were again found among the foremost, doing their duty fearlessly, and laying down their lives for the cause of liberty.

On the 3d day of July, George Washington of Virginia, having been chosen therefor by the Continental Congress, took command of the Continental army on Cambridge Common.

On the 27th of May, 1776, "the representative of the town was instructed, that, if the Honorable Congress should for the safety of the Colonies declare them independent of the kingdom of Great Britain, 'we, the said inhabitants, will solemnly engage with our lives and fortunes to support them in the measure.' This was the Declaration of Independence made, in advance of the general action, by the people of Cambridge."

As the march of time brought in their turn the centennial anniversaries of the events of 1775 above alluded to, the city of Cambridge, which, in the war of 1861–5, had given ample evidence that the memory of the men of '75 was cherished by their descendants and successors, again took an active part.

On the 19th of April, 1875, Cambridge was represented at the Lexington Centennial Celebration by Hon. JAMES D. GREEN of Ward One, Hon. JOHN SARGENT of Ward Two, Mr. SAMUEL SLOCOMB of Ward Three, Mr. JOHN LIVERMORE of Ward Four, and Mr. SOLOMON S. SLEEPER of Ward Five, as special delegates, accompanied by the MAYOR and CITY COUNCIL, and an escort comprising the

Boston Light Dragoons (a large portion of the members being citizens of Cambridge), the Fourth Battalion of Infantry M. V. M. (the members of Company B, and the Major commanding, being also Cambridge citizens), and Posts 30, 56, and 57 of the Grand Army of the Republic; while several members of the City Council, Company K, 5th Regiment M. V. M., and many citizens, joined in the celebration at Concord.

On the 17th of June, Cambridge was officially represented by His Honor Mayor BRADFORD; the military companies of the city, and several organizations, including representatives of the different manufactures and trades, joining in the splendid parade in Boston, while many thousands of the residents of Cambridge were included in the immense throng of spectators. The Cambridge City Guard (Co. K, 5th Regt. M. V. M.), having as guests the Norfolk Light Artillery Blues of Norfolk, Va., gave a banquet in the evening at Porter's Hotel, to which the City Council and many prominent citizens were invited for the purpose of meeting and extending an official welcome to the visiting company and its guests, — General FITZ HUGH LEE, who commanded a division of Confederate cavalry during the late war; Colonel WALTER H. TAYLOR, who was Adjutant-General to General Robert E. Lee; Colonel L. D. STARK, who commanded Norfolk troops; Major WILLIAM E. FOSTER, also of the Confederate army; and representatives of the "Norfolk Virginian" and "Norfolk Landmark." Pledges of renewed fealty to the Union, and hearty acceptance of such pledges, were freely exchanged; and the Washington Elm and the memory of Washington proved strong incentives to friendship between the citizens of Cambridge and their visitors from Virginia, lately so widely separated by reason of the attempt to destroy the government which he and his compeers had founded.

Meanwhile arrangements were being actively made for a proper observance of the coming centennial anniversary of

Washington's taking command of the Continental army on Cambridge Common on the 3d of July, 1775.

An order having been passed by the City Council, a Joint Special Committee was appointed as follows: —

Of the Board of Mayor and Aldermen.
His Honor ISAAC BRADFORD, Mayor;
WILLIAM L. WHITNEY,   JOHN H. LEIGHTON.

Of the Common Council.
GEORGE F. PIPER, *President;*
FRANK A. ALLEN,   WILLIAM E. DOYLE,
HIBBARD P. ROSS,   WALTER S. SWAN,
JEREMIAH MURPHY.

The following were the principal Sub-Committees: —

On Invitations and Printing.
Mayor BRADFORD, Alderman WHITNEY, and President PIPER.

Decorations.
Alderman LEIGHTON, Councilmen SWAN and MURPHY.

Music.
Councilmen ALLEN and DOYLE.

Collation.
Councilmen ROSS and SWAN.

Salutes and Illuminations.
President PIPER and Councilman DOYLE.

Children's Entertainment.
Councilmen ALLEN and SWAN.

The several sub-committees diligently performed the duties assigned them; and the proffered suggestions of several earnest and patriotic citizens were as far as possible incorporated in the general plan.

The printers of Cambridge, ever loyal, and other organizations, together with some of the more prominent manufacturers, began to make preparations for joining in the anticipated procession: but the short time intervening between the magnificent display in Boston and the proposed celebration had the effect of limiting the authority conferred upon the Committee; and it was decided to celebrate in a manner more quiet, but deemed equally appropriate for the place and occasion. In lieu of a procession, it was further decided to have an entertainment especially for the children; trusting that the exercises would fix firmly in their minds the lessons of patriotism, and a love for the memory of the heroes of 1775. To that end, the welcome offer of the active services of Mr. BENJAMIN WOODWARD was gladly accepted; and to his energetic efforts, ably seconded by Messrs. ALLEN and SWAN of the Committee, the success of that part of the exercises of the day was largely due.

At the request of the Committee, Mr. FRANCIS L. PRATT organized an effective chorus of twenty-four male voices for an evening concert on the Common, in conjunction with Edmands' Band.

The City Forester, Mr. GEORGE WASHINGTON WHITE, who for years had anxiously cared for the "Washington Elm," placed the Common in excellent condition for the comfort of the expected multitude; and a mammoth pavilion, capable of seating four thousand people, was erected almost under the shadow of the venerated and historic tree.

The lack of a hall in the immediate vicinity suitable for the enjoyment of the dinner, and expected postprandial exercises, caused the Committee to request of the authorities of Harvard College as a special favor the use of the splendid Memorial Hall, erected by the *alumni* of the college in commemoration of the virtues and deeds of those of her sons who fell in the late civil war. The following cordial response to the application was received: —

HARVARD UNIVERSITY, 15th June, 1875.

DEAR SIR, — In reply to your request, on behalf of the city of Cambridge, for the use of Memorial Hall for a public dinner on the 3d of July next, I have the honor to say that it will give the

President and Fellows of Harvard College great pleasure to have the hall used by the city on that day. They are glad that a hall built to commemorate the virtues of the sons should be used to celebrate the brave deeds of the fathers.

I am, with much respect, your obedient servant,

CHARLES W. ELIOT, *President.*

Invitations were extended to the following Federal and State officials, representatives of various organizations, and distinguished citizens; nearly all of whom were present. A few sent notes expressing their appreciation of the observance of the day, but regretting their detention by reason of illness or imperative engagement.

INVITED GUESTS.

Hon. HENRY WILSON . . . . *Vice-President of the United States.*
„ GEORGE S. BOUTWELL . *U. S. Senator from Massachusetts.*
„ HENRY L. DAWES . . . „ „ „ „
Maj.-Gen. NATHANIEL P. BANKS „ *Representative from Mass.*
Hon. E. ROCKWOOD HOAR . . „ „ „ „
„ JOHN M. S. WILLIAMS . . „ „ „ „
„ WM. WIRT WARREN . . „ *Representative elect from Mass.*
Rear-Admiral CHARLES H. DAVIS . . . . . . *United-States Navy.*
His Excellency WM. GASTON . . *Governor of Massachusetts, and Staff.*
HORACE GRAY, Esq. . *Chief Justice Sup. Jud. Court of Massachusetts.*
President CHARLES W. ELIOT, and Fellows of Harvard College.
PERCIVAL L. EVERETT, Esq. . *M. W. Grand Master of Grand Lodge of F. and A. M. of Mass., and Suite.*
Admiral HENRY KNOX THATCHER . *President of the Mass. Society of the Order of the Cincinnati.*
Hon. MARSHALL P. WILDER . *President of N. E. Historic-Genealogical Society.*
„ GEORGE WASHINGTON WARREN . . *President of Bunker-Hill-Monument Association.*
Maj.-Gen. CHARLES DEVENS, Jr. . *ex-Commander-in-Chief of the Grand Army of the Republic.*
Maj. GEORGE S. MERRILL. *Commander of Department of Massachusetts Grand Army of the Republic.*
Hon. CHARLES FRANCIS ADAMS . . . . Boston.
„ JOSIAH QUINCY . . . . „
„ CHARLES HUDSON . . . . Lexington, Mass.
„ RICHARD FROTHINGHAM . . . . Boston, Charlestown District

INTRODUCTORY.   15

Ex-Gov. Emory Washburn . . . . *Cambridge.*
Prof. Henry W. Longfellow . . . . „
„ Benjamin Pierce . . . . „
Dr. Oliver Wendell Holmes . . . . *Boston.*
Rev. Dr. Lucius R. Paige . . . . *Cambridge.*
„ William Newell . . . . „
„ Frederic H. Hedge . . . . „
Rev. Alexander McKenzie . . . . „
Hon. Estes Howe . . . . „
„ John G. Palfrey . . . . „
Henry B. Rogers, Esq. . . . . *Boston.*
James Alexander, „ . . . . *Charlotteville, Virginia.*
Winslow Warren, „ . . . . *Boston.*
John Owen, Esq. . . . . *Cambridge.*
Hon. William A. Simmons . . . . . . *Collector of Port of Boston.*
William L. Burt, Esq. . . . . . *Postmaster of Boston District.*
Hon. Samuel C. Cobb . . . . *Mayor of Boston.*
„ William H. Furber . . . . *Mayor of Somerville.*
„ J. F. C. Hyde . . . . „ „ *Newton.*
Selectmen of Town of Lexington.
„ „ „ Concord.
„ „ „ Arlington.
Chairman of Selectmen of Watertown.
„ „ „ „ Belmont.
Brig.-Gen. Edward W. Hincks . . . . *Milwaukee, Wis.*
„ Charles F. Walcott . . . . *Cambridge.*
„ Samuel E. Chamberlain . *Boston, Charlestown District.*
Capt. George A. Keeler . . . . . . *Co. K, 5th Regt. M. V. M.*
„ Levi Hawkes . . . . *Co. B, 4th Batt. M. V. M.*
Commander William P. Livesey . *Post* 30, *Dep't of Mass. G. A. R.*
„ William W. Webb . . . „ 56, „ „ „
„ Alphonso M. Lunt . . . „ 57, „ „ „
Hon. Ezra Parmenter . . *Senator from Third Middlesex District.*
Levi L. Cushing . . . *Representative from Seventh Mid. Rep. Dist.*
Daniel H. Thurston . . . „ „ *Eighth* „ „
Edward Kendall . . . . „ „ „ „ „
Austin C. Wellington . . . „ „ „ „ „
J. W. Coveney . . . . . „ „ *Ninth* „ „
Charles Kimball . . . . *Sheriff of Middlesex County.*
Hon. John S. Ladd . . . . *Justice of Police Court of Cambridge.*
Ex-Mayors of the City of Cambridge.
Ex-Presidents of the Common Council of Cambridge.

[FORM OF INVITATION.]

City of Cambridge.

The pleasure of your company is requested on Saturday, July 3rd, 1875, at the

Centennial Celebration

of Washington's assuming command of the American Army on Cambridge Common.

ISAAC BRADFORD, Mayor,
For Committee of Arrangements.

Guests will report at Lyceum Hall, Cambridge, at 11 o'clock, A. M., presenting this invitation at the door.

☞ Please reply at your earliest convenience.

THE DECORATIONS.

SUITABLE inscriptions were placed by the committee at the following points of historic interest in the city, for the information of visitors, and to freshen the recollections of citizens generally. At

THE WASHINGTON ELM,

the decorations naturally attracted great attention. A staff had been fixed in the centre of the tree, from which, high above the tallest branches, floated the American flag. Smaller flags were fastened upon all the larger projecting limbs of the tree, and extended beyond it on all sides, covering it with a perfect glory of stars and stripes. On the stone at its base, which commemorates Washington's assumption of command, was placed a life-size figure-painting of General Washington on horseback. A little in front of the elm, and so erected that the stone and painting were seen through it in perspective, was a decorated arch, under which the procession passed on the way from Lyceum Hall to the tent. The upper portion of the arch was inscribed "Birthplace of the American Army," and on the pillars were the dates "1775" and "1875."

CHRIST CHURCH.

Christ Church was decorated with flags drooping over the door and from the window in the tower. From the window also projected several flags, as well as from the corners of the tower and church. On the centre of the front was a round shield bearing this inscription : "Christ Church; erected A.D. 1780. Captain Chester's Co., from Wethersfield, Conn., was quartered here during the siege of Boston in 1775-6. Reoccupied as a house of prayer by order of General Washington, who worshipped here on Sunday, Dec. 31, 1775, and, it is believed, on subsequent occasions."

REVOLUTIONARY SOLDIERS' MONUMENT.

The monument in the Old Burial Ground erected to the Cambridge men who fell at Lexington was beautifully trimmed. It was surmounted by an arch, from which hung a flag forming a background to the monument itself. On the crown of the arch was the motto, "The Blood of the Patriots is the Seed of Liberty." On the pillars of the arch were the names of the soldiers, — Hicks, Marcy, Richardson, Russell, Wyman, and Winship.

THE COMMON.

The Soldiers' Monument on the Common was decorated with small flags. Around it, mounted, pointed in different directions, were the three cannon recently given the city by the State. They are very old pieces of ordnance; one having been captured from the French at the taking of Louisburg in 1756, and transferred to Crown Point, and then, with the others, taken from Crown Point by General Ethan Allen, "in the name of the Continental Congress," in 1775, and transferred for use at the siege of Boston.

KIRKLAND STREET.

At the junction of Kirkland Street with North Avenue was a placard stating that to be "The road to Bunker Hill, down which the troops marched under Colonel Prescott, on the evening of June 16, 1775, after prayer on the Common by President Langdon."

WASHINGTON'S HEADQUARTERS.

The poet Longfellow's house, on Brattle Street, was marked by the inscription, "Headquarters of Washington; occupied by him from July 12, 1775, to March, 1776. Built and owned at the time by John Vassal, a refugee and Tory."

THE WADSWORTH HOUSE.

The Wadsworth House, in the college-grounds facing Harvard Street, was inscribed, "Wadsworth House: first headquarters of Washington and Lee, July 2, 1775. Officers' quarters during the siege of Boston, 1775-6."

THE HOLMES HOUSE.

The house in Holmes Place, off North Avenue, near the Common, was inscribed, "Holmes House. Headquarters of General Ward. Here was held the council of war which ordered the fortification of Bunker Hill."

THE OLIVER HOUSE.

The house of James Russell Lowell, on Elmwood Avenue, bore the inscription, "Built by Andrew Oliver, stamp-commissioner and lieutenant-governor ; a refugee. Occupied as a hospital after Bunker Hill. In the field in front many soldiers were buried. Afterward the residence of Elbridge Gerry, a signer of the Declaration of Independence, Governor of Massachusetts, and Vice-President of the United States."

THE FAYERWEATHER HOUSE.

The ancient house on Brattle Street, at the corner of Fayerweather, was inscribed, "Fayerweather House; used as a hospital, 1775."

THE LEE MANSION.

The house at the corner of Brattle and Appleton Streets was marked as being the oldest building in Cambridge. It was the residence of Judge Joseph Lee, a royalist, in 1775, and is believed to have been erected before the days of Charles the Second.

THE LECHMERE HOUSE.

The old mansion on the corner of Brattle and Sparks Streets had the inscription, "Lechmere House. Baroness de Riedesel, taken prisoner with her husband at Saratoga, was lodged here."

THE BELCHER HOUSE.

The house on the corner of Brattle and Ash Streets, a structure of great antiquity, was marked by an inscription, stating that it was "Built during the reign of Queen Anne; probably by the father of Governor Belcher, who sold it in 1719. It was occupied in 1775 by Benjamin Church, M.D., Surgeon-General of the Provincial Army."

THE BRATTLE HOUSE.

The house on Brattle Street, just west of the University Press, bore the inscription, "Brattle House: residence of Thomas Brattle, Esq. Headquarters of General Mifflin."

THE APTHORP HOUSE.

The house on Harvard Street, near Plympton Street, had the inscription, "Built by East Apthorp. Called the 'Bishop's Palace.' Occupied by General Burgoyne while a prisoner."

BRADISH'S TAVERN.

An ancient building on Brighton Street, between Harvard Square and Mount-Auburn Street, was marked "Bradish's Tavern. Officers of Burgoyne's army were quartered here."

SITE OF THE INMAN HOUSE.

The site of the Inman House, on Inman Street, near Main, was inscribed, "Site of Inman House: Headquarters of General Putnam, commanding centre of American Army, July, 1775."

The college authorities had also appropriately called attention to the Revolutionary record of —

HARVARD COLLEGE.

Over the main entrance to the college-grounds, opposite Church Street, was erected an arch draped with colored bunting, and crowned by a shield bearing the motto, "Veritas." Across the top of the arch was the verse from Lowell: —

> "Life of whate'er makes life worth living,
> One heavenly thing whereof earth has the giving."

On the left pillar of the arch was the inscription, "Promote, then, as an object of primary importance, institutions for the general diffusion of knowledge. In proportion as a structure of a government gives force to public opinion, it is essential that public opinion should be enlightened. — *Washington's Farewell Address*."

On the opposite pillar was the following: "Harvard College,' — 'The Nest of Sedition.' General Gage, 1775. Hatched in this nest were James Otis, Joseph Warren, John Hancock, Josiah Quincy, Samuel Adams, Artemas Ward, Timothy Pickering, and William Eustis."

Other buildings of the college — Holden Chapel, built in 1744; Hollis Hall, built in 1763; Harvard Hall, built in 1764; and Massachusetts Hall, built in 1720 — bore inscriptions stating the date of their erection, and the fact that they were occupied by Provincial troops during the siege of Boston, 1775-6.

Dane Hall, the Law School, was inscribed, "Site of Old Church, where the first and second Provincial Congresses were held, presided over by John Hancock and Joseph Warren. General Washington worshipped in this church in 1775."

THE CITY HALL.

The City Hall was the most elaborately decorated of any building in the city. A large painting, emblematical of the victory of freedom in the Revolutionary War, hung over the front. On either side of the painting were the dates "1775" and "1875;" and at the bottom the motto,

"Liberty and Union, Now and Forever, One and Inseparable." An eagle on the centre of the roof held in his beak streamers of bunting, which draped the cornice to the corners. The painting was also draped, and the bunting so arranged as to form an immense shield covering nearly the whole front of the building, with the painting in the centre. From the flagstaff on the centre of the roof a "glory" of variously colored bunting depended to the cornice.

LYCEUM HALL.

Lyceum Hall, the headquarters of the Committee of Arrangements, was profusely trimmed. Festoons of bunting depended from the apex of the roof to the corners of the first story. On the front was a painting of the Goddess of Liberty with drawn sword, holding the stars and stripes, which was draped with flags hung from the story above. On the left side of the entrance was the motto, "Liberty, — generations past and generations to come hold us responsible for this sacred trust." On the right side was the inscription, "Warren, Hancock, Adams, Prescott. We would recall the forms and lineaments of the honored dead."

THE SITE OF FORT PUTNAM,

On the corner of Otis and Fourth Streets, was marked by a flag hung across Otis Street from the Putnam Schoolhouse, with the inscription, "Site of Fort Putnam."

FORT WASHINGTON,

Near the foot of Brookline street, was also appropriately marked, and the way to it pointed out; while from its tall flag-staff floated the largest flag in the city. The well-kept embankment, substantial iron fence, and the three cannon mounted in the embrasures as of yore, attracted much attention.

UNION-RAILWAY OFFICES.

The offices of the Union Railway were elaborately decorated. The roof was surmounted by a gilt eagle holding festoons of bunting in his beak, which drooped to either corner of the roof. From the centre also fell festoons of flags to the corners of the building on the first floor. Pennants depended from the roof in four places, and small flags projected over the street. On the front of one building was a shield with the national arms and motto. Under that was the inscription, " Mansion House of Zachariah Boardman, 1775; Tavern of Major John Brown, 1781." On the front of the other building was the name "Washington."

Flags were also freely displayed on many private residences in various parts of the city, and on all the public buildings and staffs.

A few of the citizens also displayed inscriptions or other decorations; but the lack of a procession with an extended route prevented such action being general.

NOTE.

THE " Cambridge Chronicle " of July 3d contained a lengthy illustrated article, entitled " Points of Interest," giving a detailed description of the houses and places already mentioned as having been designated by inscriptions on that day, and many historical facts connected therewith ; and also of many others necessarily omitted here, as not being directly connected with the event celebrated. But it is worthy of record, that

" The city of Cambridge to-day contains many monuments of the olden time, — many residences, lacking, perhaps, the beauty of their youth, but rich in historical reminiscence. . . . Several of the best known and best preserved are situated on Brattle Street, partially hidden from each other by the sinuosities of that ancient roadway, caused by an avoidance of the marshes then existing. But these houses were, with scarcely an exception, the homesteads of a band of royalists, connected by marriage, or direct descent, from Governor Spencer Phips. These several mansions constituted what was then called 'Church Row,' but afterwards 'Tory Row.' The owners were all men of education and fortune, and prominent attendants, several of them wardens, of Christ Church. . . . Between Arrow and Mount-Auburn Streets was the estate of David Phips, Sheriff of Middlesex, colonel of the governor's troop, and son of Governor Spencer Phips. A prominent royalist, his house, some time a hospital, was afterwards the residence of William Winthrop, and is now in a fair state of preservation. The estate is more interesting to the antiquary as being that of Daniel Gookin, Indian superintendent in the time of Eliot, and one of the licensers of the printing-press in 1662. It was under Gookin's roof, and perhaps on this very spot, that Generals Goffe and Whalley were sheltered until the news of the Restoration, and Act of Indemnity, caused them to seek another asylum.

"In the vicinity of North Avenue still remain many old residences, witnesses of the scenes of April 19th, June 17th, and July 3d; but Cambridge is so full of such places of interest, that these, having more intimate connection with the first-named dates, can receive but this passing notice. The joyous notes of this Centennial will resound as loudly within their walls as within those of their more lordly neighbors. From out their less pretentious entrances came, in the days that tried men's souls, their full proportion of patriots, to make good the vacancies caused by the defection of the royalists of Tory Row; but from many of both classes in the latter-day struggles, when the deeds of 1775 were to be repeated, so far as was necessary to maintain the life of the nation then born and baptized in blood, came forth men true to the memories of their fathers and the record of Cambridge of 1775."

THE CELEBRATION.

THE day opened bright and clear, ushered in by a sunrise salute of thirteen guns on the Common by a section of Battery A, First Battalion Light Artillery, and the ringing of bells throughout the city.

At half-past ten o'clock, ladies, and gentlemen accompanying, were admitted to the tent, and soon began to test its capacity.

At half-past eleven o'clock, the City Government and invited guests, having assembled at Lyceum Hall, formed a procession, and marched to the tent, in the following order: —

Chief of Police and Aides.
Edmands' Band.
Committee of Arrangements.
Orator, Poet, and Chaplains.
City Messenger.
Mayor and President of the Common Council.
Board of Aldermen.
Common Council.
Invited Guests, in the order previously stated.
Members of the School Committee.
Overseers of the Poor.
Board of Assessors.
Heads of Departments.
Water Board.
Cemetery Commissioners.
Commissioners of Sinking Fund.
Trustees of other Funds.
Engineers of the Fire Department.

At twelve o'clock, the procession having reached the tent, and its members being seated on the spacious platform erected therefor, the Mayor called the large audience to attention, and the exercises were begun with prayer by Rev. DAVID O. MEARS. After music by the band, Mayor BRADFORD spoke as follows: —

This day is the one hundredth anniversary of a day memorable alike in the annals of Cambridge and of the country; for it was on the third day of July, 1775, that General Washington, — then recently appointed Commander-in-Chief of the American Army, — having arrived in Cambridge from Philadelphia, here upon this hallowed ground, beneath this ancient elm-tree, unsheathed his sword, and assumed command, — a command which was to continue till the time of final victory.

To fittingly commemorate this event, so full of patriotic inspiration, we are assembled: and, as we listen to the words of our chosen orator and poet, we shall have renewed within us a sense of our large indebtedness to that lofty heroism, that self-sacrificing devotion to liberty, which accomplished an independent nation, and bequeathed to us for an inheritance that most precious of gifts, — a free republican government.

It is the name of Washington we reverence; and proud we are, among the many glorious memories of the past, of the association of his name with Cambridge.

I have the honor of introducing to you the poet of the day, Professor JAMES RUSSELL LOWELL.

POEM,

BY

JAMES RUSSELL LOWELL.

I.

1.

WORDS pass as wind, but where great deeds were done
A power abides transfused from sire to son:
The boy feels deeper meanings thrill his ear,
That tingling through his pulse life-long shall run,
With sure impulsion to keep honor clear,
When, pointing down, his father whispers, "Here,
Here, where we stand, stood he, the purely Great,
Whose soul no siren passion could unsphere,
Then nameless, now a power and mixed with fate."
Historic town, thou holdest sacred dust,
Once known to men as pious, learnëd, just,
And one memorial pile that dares to last;
But Memory greets with reverential kiss
No spot in all thy circuit sweet as this,
Touched by that modest glory as it past,
O'er which yon elm hath piously displayed
These hundred years its monumental shade.

2.

Of our swift passage through this scenery
Of life and death, more durable than we,
What landmark so congenial as a tree
Repeating its green legend every spring,
And, with a yearly ring,
Recording the fair seasons as they flee,
Type of our brief but still-renewed mortality?

We fall as leaves: the immortal trunk remains,
Builded with costly juice of hearts and brains
Gone to the mould now, whither all that be
Vanish returnless, yet are procreant still
In human lives to come of good or ill,
And feed unseen the roots of Destiny.

II.

1.

Men's monuments, grown old, forget their names
They should eternize, but the place
Where shining souls have passed imbibes a grace
Beyond mere earth; some sweetness of their fames
Leaves in the soil its unextinguished trace,
Pungent, pathetic, sad with nobler aims,
That penetrates our lives and heightens them or shames.
This unsubstantial world and fleet
Seems solid for a moment when we stand
On dust ennobled by heroic feet
Once mighty to sustain a tottering land,
And mighty still such burthen to upbear,
Nor doomed to tread the path of things that merely were:
Our sense, refined with virtue of the spot,
Across the mists of Lethe's sleepy stream
Recalls him, the sole chief without a blot,
No more a pallid image and a dream,
But as he dwelt with men decorously supreme.

2.

Our grosser minds need this terrestrial hint
To raise long-buried days from tombs of print:
"Here stood he," softly we repeat,
And lo, the statue shrined and still
In that gray minster-front we call the Past,
Feels in its frozen veins our pulses thrill,
Breathes living air and mocks at Death's deceit.
It warms, it stirs, comes down to us at last,
Its features human with familiar light.
A man, beyond the historian's art to kill,
Or sculptor's to efface with patient chisel-blight.

3.

Sure the dumb earth hath memory, nor for nought
Was Fancy given, on whose enchanted loom
Present and Past commingle, fruit and bloom
Of one fair bough, inseparably wrought
Into the seamless tapestry of thought.
So charmed, with undeluded eye we see
In history's fragmentary tale
Bright clews of continuity,
Learn that high natures over Time prevail,
And feel ourselves a link in that entail
That binds all ages past with all that are to be.

III.

1.

Beneath our consecrated elm
A century ago he stood,
Famed vaguely for that old fight in the wood
Whose red surge sought, but could not overwhelm
The life foredoomed to wield our rough-hewn helm:—
From colleges, where now the gown
To arms had yielded, from the town,
Our rude self-summoned levies flocked to see
The new-come chiefs and wonder which was he.
No need to question long; close-lipped and tall,
Long trained in murder-brooding forests lone
To bridle others' clamors and his own,
Firmly erect, he towered above them all,
The incarnate discipline that was to free
With iron curb that armed democracy.

2.

A motley rout was that which came to stare,
In raiment tanned by years of sun and storm,
Of every shape that was not uniform,
Dotted with regimentals here and there;
An army all of captains, used to pray
And still in fight, but serious drill's despair,
Skilled to debate their orders, not obey;
Deacons were there, selectmen, men of note

In half-tamed hamlets ambushed round with woods,
Ready to settle Freewill by a vote,
But largely liberal to its private moods;
Prompt to assert by manners, voice, or pen,
Or ruder arms, their rights as Englishmen,
Nor much fastidious as to how and when:
Yet seasoned stuff and fittest to create
A thought-staid army or a lasting State:
Haughty they said he was, at first, severe,
But owned, as all men own, the steady hand
Upon the bridle, patient to command,
Prized, as all prize, the justice pure from fear,
And learned to honor first, then love him, then revere:
Such power there is in clear-eyed self-restraint
And purpose clean as light from every selfish taint.

3.

Musing beneath the legendary tree,
The years between furl off: I seem to see
The sun-flecks, shaken the stirred foliage through,
Dapple with gold his sober buff and blue
And weave prophetic aureoles round the head
That shines our beacon now nor darkens with the dead.
O, man of silent mood,
A stranger among strangers then,
How art thou since renowned the Great, the Good,
Familiar as the day in all the homes of men!
The wingëd years, that winnow praise and blame,
Blow many names out: they but fan to flame
The self-renewing splendors of thy fame.

IV.

1.

How many subtlest influences unite,
With spiritual touch of joy or pain,
Invisible as air and soft as light,
To body forth that image of the brain
We call our Country, visionary shape,
Loved more than woman, fuller of fire than wine,
Whose charm can none define,

Nor any, though he flee it, can escape!
All party-colored threads the weaver Time
Sets in his web, now trivial, now sublime,
All memories, all forebodings, hopes and fears,
Mountain and river, forest, prairie, sea,
A hill, a rock, a homestead, field, or tree,
The casual gleanings of unreckoned years,
Take goddess-shape at last and there is She,
Old at our birth, new as the springing hours,
Shrine of our weakness, fortress of our powers,
Consoler, kindler, peerless 'mid her peers,
A force that 'neath our conscious being stirs,
A life to give ours permanence, when we
Are born to mingle our poor earth with hers,
And all this glowing world goes with us on our biers.

2.

Nations are long results, by ruder ways
Gathering the might that warrants length of days;
They may be pieced of half-reluctant shares
Welded by hammer-strokes of broad-brained kings,
Or from a doughty people grow, the heirs
Of wise traditions widening cautious rings;
At best they are computable things,
A strength behind us making us feel bold
In right, or, as may chance, in wrong;
Whose force by figures may be summed and told,
So many soldiers, ships, and dollars strong,
And we but drops that bear compulsory part
In the dumb throb of a mechanic heart;
But Country is a shape of each man's mind
Sacred from disenchantment, unconfined
By the cramped walls where daily drudgeries grind,
An inward vision, yet an outward birth
Of sweet familiar heaven and earth,
A brooding Presence that stirs motions blind
Of wings within our Self's beleaguering shell
That wait but her completer spell
To make us eagle-natured, fit to dare
Life's nobler spaces and untarnished air.

3.

You, who hold dear this self-conceived ideal,
Whose faith and works alone can make it real,
Bring all your fairest gifts to deck her shrine
Who lifts our lives away from Thine and Mine
And feeds the lamp of manhood more divine
With fragrant oils of quenchless constancy.
When all have done their utmost, surely he
Hath given the best who gives a character
Erect and constant, which nor any shock
Of loosened elements, nor the forceful sea
Of flowing or of ebbing fates, can stir
From its deep bases in the living rock
Of ancient manhood's sweet security :
And this he gave, serenely far from pride
As baseness, boon with prosperous stars allied,
Part of what nobler seed shall in our loins abide.

4.

No bond of men so strong as common pride
In names sublimed by deeds that have not died,
Still operant, with the primal Force allied ;
These are their arsenals, these the exhaustless mines
That give a constant heart in great designs ;
These are the stuff whereof such dreams are made
As make heroic men : thus surely he
Still holds in place the massy blocks he laid
'Neath our new frame, enforcing soberly
The self-control that makes and keeps a people free.

V.

1.

O, for a drop of that terse Roman's ink
Who gave Agricola dateless length of days,
To celebrate him fitly, neither swerve
To phrase unkempt, nor pass discretion's brink,
With him so statue-like in sad reserve,
So diffident to claim, so forward to deserve !

Nor need I shun due influence of his fame
Who, mortal among mortals, seemed as now
The equestrian shape with unimpassioned brow,
That paces silent on through vistas of acclaim.

2.

What figure more immovably august
Than that grave strength so patient and so pure,
Calm in good fortune, when it wavered, sure,
That mind serene, impenetrably just,
Modelled on classic lines so simple they endure?
That soul so softly radiant and so white
The track it left seems less of fire than light,
Cold but to such as love distemperature?
And if pure light, as some deem, be the force
That drives rejoicing planets on their course,
Why for his power benign seek an impurer source?
His was the true enthusiasm that burns long,
Domestically bright,
Fed from itself and shy of human sight,
The hidden force that makes a lifetime strong,
And not the short-lived fuel of a song.
Passionless, say you? What is passion for
But to sublime our natures and control
To front heroic toils with late return.
Or none, or such as shames the conqueror?
That fire was fed with substance of the soul
And not with holiday stubble, that could burn,
Unpraised of men who after bonfires run,
Through seven slow years of unadvancing war,
Equal when fields were lost or fields were won,
With breath of popular applause or blame,
Nor fanned nor damped, unquenchably the same,
Too inward to be reached by flaws of idle fame.

3.

Soldier and statesman, rarest unison;
High-poised example of great duties done
Simply as breathing, a world's honors worn
As life's indifferent gifts to all men born;
Dumb for himself, unless it were to God,
But for his barefoot soldiers eloquent,

Tramping the snow to coral where they trod,
Held by his awe in hollow-eyed content;
Modest, yet firm as Nature's self; unblamed
Save by the men his nobler temper shamed;
Never seduced through show of present good
By other than unsetting lights to steer
New-trimmed in Heaven, nor than his steadfast mood
More steadfast, far from rashness as from fear;
Rigid, but with himself first, grasping still
In swerveless poise the wave-beat helm of will;
Not honored then or now because he wooed
The popular voice, but that he still withstood;
Broad-minded, higher souled, there is but one
Who was all this and ours, and all men's, — WASHINGTON.

4.

Minds strong by fits, irregularly great,
That flash and darken like revolving lights,
Catch more the vulgar eye unschooled to wait
On the long curve of patient days and nights,
Rounding a whole life to the circle fair
Of orbed fulfilment; and this balanced soul,
So simple in its grandeur, coldly bare
Of draperies theatric, standing there
In perfect symmetry of self-control,
Seems not so great at first, but greater grows
Still as we look, and by experience learn
How grand this quiet is, how nobly stern
The discipline that wrought through lifelong throes
That energetic passion of repose.

5.

A nature too decorous and severe,
Too self-respectful in its griefs and joys,
For ardent girls and boys
Who find no genius in a mind so clear
That its grave depths seem obvious and near,
Nor a soul great that made so little noise.
They feel no force in that calm-cadenced phrase,
The habitual full-dress of his well-bred mind,

That seems to pace the minuet's courtly maze
And tell of ampler leisures, roomier length of days.
His firm-based brain, to self so little kind
That no tumultuary blood could blind,
Formed to control men, not amaze,
Looms not like those that borrow height of haze :
It was a world of statelier movement then
Than this we fret in, he a denizen
Of that ideal Rome that made a man for men.

VI.

1.

The longer on this earth we live
And weigh the various qualities of men,
Seeing how most are fugitive,
Or fitful gifts, at best, of now and then,
Wind-wavered corpse-lights, daughters of the fen,
The more we feel the high stern-featured beauty
Of plain devotedness to duty,
Steadfast and still, nor paid with mortal praise,
But finding amplest recompense
For life's ungarlanded expense
In work done squarely and unwasted days.
For this we honor him, that he could know
How sweet the service and how free
Of her, God's eldest daughter here below,
And choose in meanest raiment which was she.

2.

Placid completeness, life without a fall
From faith or highest aims, truth's breachless wall,
Surely if any fame can bear the touch,
His will say " Here ! " at the last trumpet's call,
The unexpressive man whose life expressed so much.

VII.

1.

Never to see a nation born
Hath been given to mortal man,
Unless to those who, on that summer morn,
Gazed silent when the great Virginian
Unsheathed the sword whose fatal flash
Shot union through the incoherent clash
Of our loose atoms, crystallizing them
Around a single will's unpliant stem,
And making purpose of emotion rash.
Out of that scabbard sprang, as from its womb,
Nebulous at first but hardening to a star,
Through mutual share of sunburst and of gloom,
The common faith that made us what we are.

2.

That lifted blade transformed our jangling clans,
Till then provincial, to Americans,
And made a unity of wildering plans;
Here was the doom fixed: here is marked the date
When this New World awoke to man's estate,
Burnt its last ship and ceased to look behind:
Nor thoughtless was the choice; no love or hate
Could from its poise move that deliberate mind,
Weighing between too early and too late
Those pitfalls of the man refused by Fate:
His was the impartial vision of the great
Who see not as they wish, but as they find.
He saw the dangers of defeat, nor less
The incomputable perils of success;
The sacred past thrown by, an empty rind;
The future, cloud-land, snare of prophets blind;
The waste of war, the ignominy of peace;
On either hand a sullen rear of woes,
Whose garnered lightnings none could guess,
Piling its thunder-heads and muttering "Cease!"
Yet drew not back his hand, but gravely chose
The seeming-desperate task whence our new nation rose.

3.

A noble choice and of immortal seed!
Nor deem that acts heroic wait on chance
Or easy were as in a boy's romance;
The man's whole life preludes the single deed
That shall decide if his inheritance
Be with the sifted few of matchless breed,
Our race's sap and sustenance,
Or with the unmotived herd that only sleep and feed.
Choice seems a thing indifferent; thus or so,
What matters it? The Fates with mocking face
Look on inexorable, nor seem to know
Where the lot lurks that gives life's foremost place.
Yet Duty's leaden casket holds it still,
And but two ways are offered to our will,
Toil with rare triumph, ease with safe disgrace,
The problem still for us and all of human race.
He chose, as men choose, where most danger showed,
Nor ever faltered 'neath the load
Of petty cares, that gall great hearts the most,
But kept right on the strenuous uphill road,
Strong to the end, above complaint or boast:
The popular tempest on his rock-mailed coast
Wasted its wind-borne spray,
The noisy marvel of a day;
His soul sate still in its unstormed abode.

VIII.

Virginia gave us this imperial man
Cast in the massive mould
Of those high-statured ages old
Which into grander forms our mortal metal ran;
She gave us this unblemished gentleman:
What shall we give her back but love and praise
As in the dear old unestrangèd days
Before the inevitable wrong began?
Mother of States and undiminished men,
Thou gavest us a country, giving him,

And we owe alway what we owed thee then:
The boon thou wouldst have snatched from us agen
Shines as before with no abatement dim.
A great man's memory is the only thing
With influence to outlast the present whim
And bind us as when here he knit our golden ring.
All of him that was subject to the hours
Lies in thy soil and makes it part of ours:
Across more recent graves,
Where unresentful Nature waves
Her pennons o'er the shot-ploughed sod,
Proclaiming the sweet Truce of Gód,
We from this consecrated plain stretch out
Our hands as free from afterthought or doubt
As here the united North
Poured her embrownëd manhood forth
In welcome of our savior and thy son.
Through battle we have better learned thy worth,
The long-breathed valor and undaunted will,
Which, like his own, the day's disaster done,
Could, safe in manhood, suffer and be still.
Both thine and ours the victory hardly won;
If ever with distempered voice or pen
We have misdeemed thee, here we take it back,
And for the dead of both don common black.
Be to us evermore as thou wast then,
As we forget thou hast not always been,
Mother of States and unpolluted men,
Virginia, fitly named from England's manly queen!

After another selection by the band, Mayor BRADFORD introduced Rev. ANDREW P. PEABODY, D.D., the orator of the day.

[NOTE. — The Poem by Prof. LOWELL (as well as that by Dr. HOLMES) is here printed "by permission of H. O. Houghton & Co., publishers of the 'Atlantic Month'y.'" with alterations and additional lines.]

ADDRESS,

BY

REV. ANDREW P. PEABODY, D.D.

WHEN it was proposed to give a place to this epoch in the series of centennials, my first thought was that Lexington, Concord, Bunker Hill, in so recent memory, and the already glowing work of preparation for the country's hundredth birthday, would so dwarf and chill our celebration here as to make it merely a heartless municipal parade. But the occasion has grown upon me. I see and feel that it holds the foremost place in the series. It has paramount claims, not on us or our State, but on our whole people. We might rightfully have made our arrangements, not for a local, but for a national festival. We commemorate the epoch but for which Lexington, Concord, Bunker Hill, would have left in our history hardly a trace, probably not a single name, and the centennial of our independence would remain for a generation not yet upon the stage to celebrate.

Cambridge was the first capital of our infant republic, the cradle of our nascent liberty, the hearth of our kindling patriotism. Before the 3d of July, 1775, there were tumults, conflicts, bold plans, rash enterprises; but there was no co-ordinating and controlling will, purpose, or authority. On and from that day the colonies were virtually one people. Before, they had nothing in common but their grievances. They were as yet British provinces; though wrenching the cords that held them, still undetached, and with no mode of action upon or with one another. By adopting the army, and choosing its head, they performed their first act, not of alliance, but of organic unity, and became a nation unawares, while they thought themselves still wronged and suppliant dependencies of the British crown. They thus decided the question between a worse than unsuccessful rebellion and revolution.

That the rebellion, as such, would have been an utter failure, is only too certain. The American party in England had on its side eloquence indeed, and wisdom, but neither numerical force in parliament, nor the power to mollify ministerial obstinacy, or to penetrate with a sense of right the gross stupidity on the throne. Boston was held by disciplined, thoroughly armed, and well-fed troops, under officers of approved skill and prowess, strongly intrenched and fortified at accessible points, and sustained by a formidable naval force. Hardly one in fifty of the colonial army had had any experience in war; and I doubt whether there was a single man among them, officer or private, who was a soldier by profession. They had come from the farm and the forge, with such arms and equipments as they could bring: they had no bureau of supply, no military chest, nor organized commissariat; and their stock of ammunition was so slender, that it was ordered by the Provincial Congress that no salute should be fired on the reception of the commander-in-chief. They were from four different provinces, under as many generals, with sectional jealousies which the common cause could hardly keep at bay; and harmonious counsels could be maintained or expected only and scarcely at moments of imminent peril. At Bunker Hill they had shown both their strength and their weakness, their unsurpassed courage and their poverty of resource. Superior in the conflict, overwhelming the enemy with the shame and disaster of a signal defeat, they had been compelled to yield the ground on which they had won imperishable glory, and to see the heights they had so bravely defended occupied by a hostile battery. They held Boston beleaguered by the prestige of that day, too feeble to press the siege, yet, as they had well proved, too strong to be dislodged and scattered but by the disintegrating elements in their own unorganized body. These elements were already at work, and the secession of even a single regiment would have been the signal for speedy dissolution, and submission to the royal government.

This precarious condition of affairs was beyond the remedial authority of the individual provinces. Massachusetts could choose a general for her own troops, but could not place the forces of New Hampshire, Connecticut, and Rhode Island, under his control. Still less could any efficient system of sustenance or armament have been arranged by several legislatures. A central authority alone could carry forward the resistance so nobly begun. The Continental Congress would in vain have passed patriotic resolutions, protests against tyranny, votes of sympathy ; in vain would they have aroused popular indignation and multiplied centres of resistance through the land. The one decisive act in the struggle, the seal of what had been achieved, the presage and pledge of all that should ensue in the coming years, was that the consummation of which we now celebrate.

Cambridge was for obvious geographical reasons the only place where the provincial troops could have their head-quarters, — lying near enough to the enemy to watch and check his movements, yet protected from sudden or insidious attack by the intervention of the then unbridged arm of the sea which separates it from Boston. There was, at the same time, an intrinsic fitness that the opening scenes of the great drama should be enacted here, where so many of the leaders in counsel and arms had learned to loathe oppression and to hold the cause of liberty sacred.

From its earliest days our university had always been on the side of freedom. Its first two presidents were far in advance of their times in their views of the right of the individual man to unrestricted liberty of thought, opinion, speech, and action. Increase Mather, when president, took the lead in the opposition to the tyrannical acts of Andros and Randolph, sailed for England as the unofficial agent of the aggrieved colonists, was appointed to an official agency on the news of the revolution of 1688, bore an important part in the construction of the new provincial charter and in securing its acceptance, and nominated to the royal court the governor, council, and principal officers under it. His successors were of a like spirit; and there is on record no instance in which the college succumbed to usurpation, stooped to sycophancy, or maintained other than an erect position before the emissaries of the royal government. The culture of the students was in great part classical, and in the last century the classics were the text-books of all lovers of freedom. A sceptical criticism had not then cast doubt on any of the stories of ancient heroism; nor had a minute analysis laid bare the excesses and defects of the early republics, whose statesmen and warriors were deemed the peerless models of patriotic virtue, and whose orators thrilled the hearts of their New-England readers as they had the Athenian *demos*, the senate in the capitol, or the dense masses of Roman citizens in the forum.

Almost all the Massachusetts clergy, perhaps the major part of those of New England, had been educated here. The Tories among them were very few, and nearly the whole of their number were ardent patriots. The pulpit then sustained in affairs of public moment the part which is now borne by the daily press; its utterances during the eventful years of our life-struggle had no uncertain sound; and the champions, deeds of prowess, and war-lyrics of the Hebrew Scriptures gave the frequent key-note to sermon, prayer, and sacred song.

Among the pioneers and guiding spirits of the Revolution who were graduates of the college, when I have named the Adamses, Otises, Quincys, Warrens, Pickering, Hancock, Trumbull, Ward, Cushing,

Bowdoin, Phillips, I have but given you specimens of the type and temper of those who for many years had gone from Cambridge to fill the foremost places of trust and influence throughout and beyond our Commonwealth. That they carried with them hence their liberal views of government and of the rights of man, we well know in the case of those of whose lives we have the record. Thus we find John Adams, just after graduating here, more than twenty years before the declaration of independence, writing to a friend his anticipations for America, not only of her freedom from European sway, but of her becoming the chief seat of empire for the world. Year after year, on the commencement platform in the old parish-church, had successive ranks of earnest young men rehearsed to greedy ears the dream of liberty which they pledged faith and life to realize.

In the successive stages of the conflict of the colonies with the mother-country, the college uniformly committed itself unequivocally on the patriotic side. When the restrictions on the colonial trade called forth warm expressions of resentment, the senior class unanimously resolved to take their degrees in what must then have been exceedingly rude apparel, — home-spun and home-made cloth. When tea was proscribed by public sentiment, and some few students persisted in bringing it into' commons, the faculty forbade its use, alleging that it was a source of grief and uneasiness to many of the students, and that banishing it was essential to harmony and peace within the college-walls. After the day of Lexington and Concord all four of the then existing college-buildings were given up for barracks, and the president's house for officers' quarters. When the commander-in-chief was expected, this house was designated for his use, with the reservation of a single room for President Langdon's own occupancy. Though the few remaining students were removed to Concord, the president, an ardent patriot, seems to have still resided here, or at least to have spent a large portion of his time near the troops; for we find frequent traces of his presence among them, and on the eve of the battle of Bunker Hill he officiated as their chaplain. In connection with the prevailing spirit of the university, it is worthy of emphatic statement that the commander-in-chief was the first person who here received the honorary degree of doctor of laws.

To Harvard graduates the country was indebted for the choice of the illustrious chieftain. The earliest mention that we can find of Washington's name in this connection is in a letter of James Warren to John Adams, bearing date the 7th of May. Adams seems at once to have regarded him as the only man fitted for this momentous service. Though the formal nomination was made by Mr. Johnson of Maryland, Mr. Adams on a previous day first designated Washington as "a gentleman whose skill and experience as an officer, whose independent fortune, great talents, and excellent universal character, would command the approbation of all America, and unite the cordial exertions of all the colonies better than any other person in the Union." There were, however, objections on sectional grounds and personal ambitions that required the most delicate treatment; and it was mainly in consequence of Mr. Adams's strong will, untiring effort, and skilful handling of opposing wishes and claims, that the final ballot was unanimous. On the 5th of June the election was made. It was formally announced to Washington by Hancock, the President of Congress, and was accepted on the spot.

The commander, impressed with the imminence of the crisis, denied himself the sad privilege of a farewell in person to his own household, took leave of his wife in a letter equally brave and tender, and on the 21st commenced his northward journey. Twenty miles from Philadelphia he met a courier with tidings of the battle of Bunker Hill. Eagerly inquiring as to the details of the transaction, and learning the promptness, skill, and courage that had made the day for ever memorable, he exclaimed, "The liberties of the country are safe!" A deputation from the Provincial Congress met him at Springfield, and volunteer cavalcades gave him honorable attendance from town to town, till on the 2d of July he arrived at Watertown, received and returned the congratulatory address of the Congress there assembled, and was then escorted by a company of horse and a goodly body of mounted civilians to the president's house, now known as Wadsworth House. The rapid journey on horseback from Philadelphia to Cambridge, and that in part over rough roads, — an enterprise beyond the easy conception of our time, — must have rendered the brief repose of that midsummer night essential to the prestige of the morrow, when on the first impressions of the hour may have been poised the destiny of the nation.

There were reasons why Washington not only might

have been, but would inevitably have been, ill received had he not been made to win men's confidence and love. Several of the officers already on the ground had shown their capacity for great things, and had their respective circles of admirers, who were reluctant to see them superseded by a stranger ; and, had not the officers themselves manifested a magnanimity equal to their courage, the camp would have been already distracted by hostile factions. Then, too, the Virginian and New-England character, manners, style of speech, modes of living, tastes, aptitudes, had much less in common at that time of infrequent intercourse than half a century later, when, as we well know, apart from political divergence, mere social differences were sufficient to create no little mutual repugnancy. Washington was also well known to be an Episcopalian; and Episcopacy, from the first offensive on Puritan soil, was never more abhorred than now, when its Northern professors, with hardly an exception, were openly hostile to the cause of the people; when in Cambridge almost every conspicuous dwelling, from Fresh Pond to the Inman House in Cambridgeport, had been the residence of a refugee royalist member of the English Church.

The morning of the 3d of July witnessed on the Cambridge Common, and at every point of view in and upon the few surrounding houses, such a multitude of men, women, and children, as had never been gathered here before, and perhaps has never since assembled till this very day. Never was the advent or presence of mortal man a more complete and transcendent triumph. Majestic grace and sweet benignity were blended in countenance and mien. He looked at once the hero, patriot, sage. With equal dignity and modesty he received the thunders of acclamation, in which every voice bore part. His first victory, the prestige of which forsook him not for a moment during the weary years that followed, was already gained when under yon ancient elm he drew his sword as commander-in-chief. He had conquered thousands of hearts, that remained true to him to their last throb. The wife of John Adams writes of his appearance at that moment, "Those lines of Dryden instantly occurred to me: —

> ' Mark his majestic fabric! He's a temple
> Sacred by birth, and built by hands divine;
> His soul's the deity that lodges there;
> Nor is the pile unworthy of the god.' "

Never indeed can the temple have been more worthy of the tenant. He was forty-three years of age, in the prime of manly vigor and beauty, tall and commanding, symmetrical and graceful, unsurpassed as an accomplished equestrian, with the bearing and manners of a high-bred gentleman. His countenance — in later years, and in many of the portraits and engravings of him, fearfully distorted by one of the first rude essays of American manufacturing dentistry — still bore the perfect outlines which nature gave it, and betokened the solemn grandeur of soul, loftiness, gentleness, simplicity, benevolence, which dwelt within. Peale's portrait of him, taken a year or two earlier, and engraved for the second volume of Irving's "Life of Washington," fully justifies the enthusiastic admiration which welcomed his appearance here, and in subsequent years made his mere presence an irresistible power.

With characteristic promptness he lingered not to satisfy the eyes that feasted on him, but immediately made his inspection of the encampments scattered in a semicircle from Winter Hill to Dorchester Neck, and reconnoitred the British troops from all available points of observation. On the British side he saw every token of military science, skilful engineering, and strict discipline; within the American lines, an aggregation rather than an army, — bodies of raw, untrained militia, a sad deficiency of arms, accoutements, and even necessary clothing, rudely constructed works, extensive, too, beyond the capacity of the troops to maintain and defend them. Only among the Rhode-Island regiments, under General Greene, did he discover aught of military order, system, discipline, and subordination. The greater part of the forces consisted of Massachusetts men, and these were the most destitute. The commander's large-hearted sympathy did ample justice to their need and to their patriotism. "This unhappy and devoted province," he writes to the President of Congress, " has been so long in a state of anarchy, and the yoke has been laid so heavily on it, that great allowances are to be made for troops raised under such circumstances. The deficiency of numbers, discipline, and stores can only lead to this conclusion, that their spirit has exceeded their strength."

How long Washington remained in the president's house cannot be ascertained, — probably but a few days. The house, considerably smaller than it now is, was insufficient for the accommodation of his military family; and arrangements were early made for his removal to the Vassall House, now Mr. Longfellow's, which had been deserted by its Tory owner, and occupied by the Marblehead troops. Here he resided till the following April.

I have described the acclamations of joy, trust, and hope that hailed our chieftain's arrival. With the shouts of the multitude ascended to heaven the last breath of a Cambridge patriot. Colonel Gardner — a member of the Provincial Congress, a man universally honored and beloved, a pillar in Church and State, one of the bravest officers at Bunker Hill — received his fatal wound at the head of his regiment, rallied strength to urge them to valiant and vigorous resistance, lingered death-bound till the morning that gave the troops their leader and the country its father, and left the charge of a gallant officer's obsequies for the commander's first official duty. We have the general order, bearing date July 4, for the rendering of the usual military honors at the funeral of one who — so the document reads — "fought, bled, and died in the cause of his country and mankind," — words then first used, and which have become too trite for repetition, simply because they are in themselves, beyond comparison, comprehensive, appropriate, majestic, worthy of the great heart that sought expression in them.

Washington's life here has left few records except those which belong to the history of the war and of the country. He lived generously, though frugally; receiving often at dinner his generals, the foremost personages in civil office and influence, delegates from the Continental Congress, and distinguished visitors to the camp. His own habits were almost abstemious; and when, according to the invariable custom of the time, a long session at table seemed inevitable, he left his guests in charge of some one of his staff more disposed than himself to convivial indulgence. During the latter portion of his sojourn here, his wife relieved him in part from the cares of the hospitality which she was admirably fitted to adorn. He generally attended worship at the church of the First Parish. I well remember the site of the square pew, under the shadow of the massive pulpit, which he was said to have statedly occupied; and the mention of it recalls to my recollection a couplet of a hymn written by Rev. Dr. Holmes, and sung in the old church on the Fourth of July, fifty years ago, in which he describes that house of worship as the place

> "Where, in our country's darkest day,
> Her war-clad hero came to pray."

Once, perhaps oftener, service was performed in Christ Church, whose rector and most of his leading parishioners had become exiles on political grounds.

It is impossible to overestimate the importance of these nine months in Cambridge. Washington himself was impatient of the delay. But for the prudent counsels of the generals who knew their men better than he could know them thus early, he would have made a direct assault on the British troops, and attempted to force their surrender or retreat; and it was here that he learned to wait, to curb his native impetuousness of temper, and to make discretion the trusty satellite of valor.

Meanwhile the army was constantly increasing in numbers, and was largely recruited from the Middle and Southern States; while in New England, as the term of service for which enlistments had been made expired, the soldiers either re-enlisted, or were replaced, or more than replaced, by men of equal zeal and courage. There were sufficiently frequent alarms and skirmishes to keep alive the practice of arms; while the long line of outposts, more or less exposed to sudden assault, demanded incessant vigilance, and formed a training-school in strict discipline, prompt obedience, and those essential habits of camp-life which the citizen-soldier, however brave in battle, finds most uncongenial, harassing, and burdensome.

The power of a single organizing mind was never more fully manifested than in the creation of a regular and disciplined army from the raw recruits, the materials heterogeneous to the last degree, to all appearance hopelessly incongruous, which now came under the commander's shaping hand. Confusion crystallized into order; discord resolved itself into harmony; jarring counsels were reconciled; rivalries vanished, as every man found his abilities recognized, his fitting place and due honor accorded to him, and his services utilized to their utmost capacity.

Never in the history of military achievements was there a more signal triumph than in the termination of the siege of Boston. On the morning of the 5th of March, when General Howe saw the four strong redoubts which had risen on Dorchester Heights while he slept, he exclaimed, "The rebels have done more work in one night than my whole army could have done in one month." In the evening the British were secure within their lines, and counted on the speedy dispersion of the besieging army; in the morning they saw surrender or flight as their only alternative. The siege was made complete and impregnable. But for the ships at anchor in the harbor, the entire British army would have been prisoners of war.

Thus closed the first act of the great drama, — here, where we stand, initiated, matured, directed, borne on to its glorious and ever-memorable issue. Ours, then, is more than a battle-ground, — a soil hallowed by those wise, stern, self-denying counsels, without which feats of arms were mere child's play, made sacred by the presence of such a constellation of patriots as can hardly ever, elsewhere upon earth, have deliberated on the destiny of a nation in its birth-throes, — Putnam, Greene, Stark, Prescott, Ward, Read, and their illustrious associates, men who staked their all in the contest, and deemed death for their country but a nobler and more enduring life.

Enough of history. Let us now gather up as we may some few traits of the character of him on whom our central regard is fixed in these commemorative rites.

The Washington of the popular imagination, nay, of our gravest histories, is a mythical personage, such as never lived or could have lived among men. The figure is too much like that of the perfect goddess born from the brain of Jupiter. Washington undoubtedly grew as other men grow, was not exempt from human passions and infirmities, was shaped and trained by the Providence whose chosen instrument he was. It was his glory that he yielded to the plastic hand, obeyed the heavenly vision, followed without halting the guiding spirit. The evident coldness of the Virginia delegates in Congress with regard to his appointment shows that up to that time, notwithstanding his early military experience, they had seen little in him to distinguish him from other respectable gentlemen of faultless lineage, fair estate, and unblemished reputation. But, from the moment when he accepted the command of the army, he gave himself entirely and irrevocably to his country. Such singleness of purpose as his is the essence of genius, whose self-creating law is, "This one thing I do." From that moment no collateral interest turned him aside; no shadow of self crossed his path; no lower ambition came between him and his country's cause: he had no hope, no fear, but for the sacred trust devolved upon him. His disinterestedness gave him his clear and keen vision, his unswerving impartiality, his uncompromising rectitude, his power over other minds. The self-seeking man sees double; and we learn from the highest authority that it is only when the eye is single that "the whole body is full of light." The secret of influence, also, lies here. The man who can be supposed to have personal ends in view, even though in his own mind they are but secondary, is always liable to be judged by them, and the good that is in him gains not half the confidence it deserves. But self-abnegation, when clearly recognized, wins not only respect, but assent and deference: its opinions have the validity of absolute truth; its will, the force of impersonal law. The professed philanthropists and reformers who have swarmed in the social history of the last half-century furnish a manifold illustration of this principle. The few of them who have carried large numbers along with them and have moved the world have not been the greatest and most gifted among them, but those who have cared not, if the wheel would only turn, whether it raised them to fame, or crushed them to powder. So men believed and trusted in Washington, not merely because he was a wise and prudent man, but because they knew him to be as utterly incapable of selfish aims and motives as the Liberty whose cause he served.

I have spoken of a sort of mythical, superhuman grandeur in which Washington has been enshrined in much of our popular speech and literature. I think that, on the other hand, there has been in some quarters a disposition to underrate him. For this there is ample reason, yet no ground. He seems the less because he was so great. A perfect sphere looks smaller than one of the same dimensions with a diversified surface. We measure eminences by depressions, the height of mountains by the chasms that yawn beneath them. Littlenesses of character give prominence to what there is in it of greatness. The one virtue looms up with a fascinating grandeur from a life full of faults. The patriot who will not pay his debts or govern his passions often attracts more homage than if he led a sober and honest life. The single traits of erratic genius not infrequently gain in splendor from their relief against a background of weaknesses and follies.

We might enumerate in Washington various traits of mind and character, either of which in equal measure would suffice for the fame of a man who had little else that challenged approval. But what distinguishes Washington pre-eminently is, that it is impossible to point out faults or deficiencies that marred his work, detracted from his reputation, dishonored his life. The most observed and best known man in the country for the eight years of the war, and for the other eight of his presidency, even jealousy and partisan rancor could find no pretence for the impeachment of his discretion or his virtue. His biographers have seemed to revel in the narrative of some two or three occasions on which he was intensely angry; as if, like the vulnerable heel of Achilles, they were needed to show that their hero was still human.

But let it not be forgotten that this roundness of moral proportions, this utter lack of picturesque diversity, in his character, must have been the outcome of strenuous self-discipline. His almost unruffled calmness and serenity were the result, not of apathy, but of self-conquest. It was the fierce warfare and decisive victory within that made him the cynosure of all eyes, and won for him the homage of all hearts that loved their country. We know but little of the details of his private life for the first forty years or more; but even the reverence of posterity has not succeeded in wholly veiling from view the undoubted fact that he was by nature vehement, impulsive, headstrong, impatient, passionate, — a man in whose blood the fiery coursers might easily have run riot, and strewed their way with havoc. By far the greater honor is due to him who so held them under bit, rein, and curb, that masterly self-control under intensest provocation became his foremost characteristic; that disappointment, delay, defeat, even treachery, so seldom disturbed his equanimity, spread a cloud over his brow, or drew from him a resentful or bitter word.

We admire also in him the even poise with which he bore his high command in war and in the councils of the nation. In mien, manner, speech, intercourse, he was never beneath, and never above, his place. Dignity without haughtiness, firmness without obstinacy, condescension without stooping, gentleness without suppleness, affability without undue familiarity, were blended in him as in hardly any other historical personage. No one who could claim his ear was repelled; yet to no one did he let himself down. He sought and received advice, gave its full weight and worth to honest dissent, yet never for a moment resigned the leader's staff. The more thoroughly we study the history of the war, the more manifest is it that on this one man more than on all beside depended its successful end. Congress lacked equally power and promptness; the State legislatures were dilatory, and often niggardly, in provision for their troops; exposure and privation brought portions of the army to the very brink of revolt and secession; cabals were raised in behalf of generals of more brilliant parts and more boastful pretensions; success repeatedly hovered over his banner, only to betray him in the issue: yet in every emergency he was none the less the tower of strength, or rather the guiding pillar of the nation by day and night, in cloud and fire. Heart and hope never once forsook him, and his elastic courage sustained failing hearts and rekindled flickering hope. His judgment of men, his keen insight into character, has also its prominent place among the sources of his power. In Arnold indeed, and to some degree in Gates, he was deceived; but, from the many in whom he reposed confidence, it is hard to add to the list of those who betrayed his trust. He recognized instantly the signal merit of Greene, and employed him constantly in the most arduous and responsible service. Putnam, and the other brave and devoted but untrained generals whom he found here on his arrival, lost nothing in his regard by their rusticity of garb and mien. Pickering, than whom the annals of our State bear the name of no more ardent patriot or more honorable man, was successively his secretary, commissary-general, and quarter-master, and held in his presidency, at one time or another, the chief place in almost every department of the public service. In Hamilton's very boyhood he discovered the man who eclipsed his own military fame by repairing the nation's shattered credit, and establishing her financial safety and efficiency. He understood every man's capacity, and knew how to utilize it to the utmost. Rarest gift of all, he knew what he could not do, and what others could do better than himself; and he in no respect appears greater than in committing to the most secure and efficient agency the several portions of his military and civil responsibility, in accepting whatever service might redound to the public good, and in the unstinted recognition of such service.

Time fails me, and so it would were my minutes hours, to complete the picture. Nor is there need; for lives there an American who owns not his primacy, in war, in peace, in command, in service, in uncorrupt integrity, in generous self-devotion, in loyalty to freedom, his country, and his God? Among the dead, the heroes and statesmen of all times and lands, his mighty shade rises pre-eminent, — his name the watchword of liberty, right, and law, revered wherever freedom is sought or cherished, the tyrant's rebuke, the demagogue's shame, the patriot's synonyme for untarnished fame and unfading glory.

This season of commemoration has its voices, not only of gratitude and gladness, but equally of admonition, it may be of reproach. Our nation owes its existence, its constitution, its early union, stability, progress, and prosperity, under the Divine Providence, to the great, wise, and good men who built our ship of state, and stood at its helm in the straits and among the shoals and quicksands through which it sailed into the open sea. Where are now our Washingtons, Adamses, Hamiltons, Jays, Pickerings? — the men whom a sovereign's ransom could not bribe, or a people's adulation beguile, or the lure of ambition dazzle and pervert. Nature cannot have grown niggardly of her noble births, God of his best gifts. But where are they? Unset jewels for the most part, and incapable of finding a setting under our present political *régime*. Of what avail is it that we heap honors on the illustrious fathers of our republic, if we are at no pains to seek, for their succession, heirs of their talents and their virtues? Yet, were Washington now living, — the very man of whose praise we are never weary, — does any one suppose it possible for him to be chosen to the chief magistracy? Would he answer the questions, make the compromises, give the pledges, without which no national convention would nominate him? Could he creep through the tortuous mole-paths through which men now crawl into place and grovel into power? Would he mortgage, expressly or tacitly, the vast patronage of government for the price of his election?

We sometimes hear the cry, " Not men, but measures." But, if there be any one lesson taught us by our early history, it is that men, not measures, created, saved, exalted, our nation. Corrupt men vitiate, mean men debase, dishonest men pervert; incompetent men neutralize, the best measures, if such measures be even possible, except as originated, directed, actualized, by the best men. Our rowers have now brought us into waters where there are no soundings. It is impossible to know, in the absence of a definite standard of value, whether our national wealth is increasing or declining; whether we are on the ninth wave of towering prosperity, or on the verge of general bankruptcy. It is an ominous fact, that an immense proportion of individual wealth is public debt. Never was there so much need as now of the profoundest wisdom, and an integrity beyond bribe, to crystallize our chaos, to disentangle the complexities of our situation, to disinthrall our industries from legislation which protects by cramping and crippling, to retrench the spoils of office, enormous when not exceeding legal limits, unmeasured beyond them, and through the entire hierarchy of place and trust to establish honesty and competency, not partisan zeal and efficiency, as the essential qualifications.

There is a sad and disheartening element in the pomp and splendor, the lofty panegyric and fervent eulogy, of these centennial celebrations. It was once said in keen reproach by Him who spake as never man spake, " Ye build the tombs of the prophets, and garnish the sepulchres of the righteous." It is, in general, not the age which makes history that writes it, — not the age which builds monuments that merits them. It is in looking back to a past better than the present that men say, " There were giants in those days." Reverence and gratitude for a worthy ancestry characterize, indeed, not unworthy descendants: praise and adulation of ancestors beyond reason or measure denote a degenerate posterity. Our fathers have done little for us if their equals do not now fill their places. Unless their lineage be undebased, their heritage is of little value.

Fellow-citizens, let us praise our fathers by becoming more worthy of them. Let this season of commemoration be a revival-season of public and civic virtue. Let the blessed memories which we rejoice to keep ever green be enwreathed afresh with high resolve and earnest endeavor to transmit the liberty so dearly purchased to centuries yet to come. When another centennial rolls round, let there be names identified with this, our country's second birth-time, that shall find fit place in the chaplet of honor which our children will weave. Some such names will be there, — Lincoln, Andrew, the heroes of our civil conflict, the men whose prudent counsels and diplomatic

skill in that crisis warded off worse perils than those
of armed rebellion. Let these be re-enforced by yet
other names that shall be written indelibly on the pillars of our reconstructed Union. Fellow-citizens,
heirs of renowned fathers, look to it that in your hands
their trust be fulfilled, — that the travail of their soul
have the only recompense they sought.

THE DINNER.

At the close of Dr. Peabody's address, the City Government and guests proceeded in the same order as before to Memorial Hall, which was reached at a quarter before three o'clock; and, the doors of the magnificent dining-hall being thrown open, the holders of tickets, including many ladies, entered, and took seats at the tables. Five long tables, extending the length of the hall, were laden with a sumptuous dinner, provided by John P. Farmer, Jr., steward of the hall, and were ornamented with a profusion of elegant bouquets; and the hall itself was ornamented with pot-plants, hanging-baskets, and trailing vines; while from every side the painted and sculptured portraits of scores of distinguished officers or benefactors of the University looked down upon the festive scene.

After the divine blessing had been asked by Rev. Asa Bullard, an hour was spent in enjoying the good things set before them; the band, which was stationed in the west gallery, meanwhile, and subsequently at frequent intervals, enlivening the exercises with music.

At the close of the dinner, Mayor Bradford called the company to order, and spoke briefly as follows: —

OPENING ADDRESS OF HIS HONOR MAYOR
BRADFORD.

LADIES AND GENTLEMEN, — By the kind courtesy of the college authorities, we have met here in Memorial Hall to complete the official ceremonies of the day. It is unnecessary for me to enlarge upon the memorable event which we to-day commemorate. We have listened to the inspiring words of our poet and orator; have had recalled the circumstances attending the assumption of command of the army by Washington, with the leading events of that period, so full of interest to us, the inheritors of their successes; have added one to the glorious round of centennials; and, in so doing, have rekindled within ourselves that spirit which actuated our patriot fathers. Having those present with us this afternoon, who, by word and deed, have been rendered illustrious in civil and military life, and hoping that remarks may be elicited from them adding further to the interest of the occasion, I now have the pleasure to introduce to you, as toast-master, the Hon. GEORGE P. SANGER, of this city.

Mr. SANGER said, —

MR. MAYOR, — In response to your call, I shall add nothing with any particular words of my own, except to read the regular toasts that have been prepared for the occasion, and to call upon those who are expected to respond to them.

The toast-master then announced the toasts, and responses were made as given below.

1. *"The Memory of Washington."*

In response, the company rose, and remained standing while the band played the Prayer from "Medea."

2. "*The United States of America.*"

RESPONSE BY HON. GEORGE S. BOUTWELL,

United-States Senator from Massachusetts.

Mr. Mayor, — It is a fortunate incident, as well as a great fact, in the history of this ancient town, that here Washington, the most important man of the Revolution and the greatest personage in American history, took command of the colonial forces. It was the first great fact in our history which showed forth the purpose of the people to vindicate, first, their rights as Englishmen ; and, having so vindicated their rights, to establish a government in which those rights should be recognized, confirmed, and perpetuated by the supreme, vigilant, and constantly exercised power of the people. The first of our historians has said in private, and in one of the most charming chapters of his history has also plainly declared, that Washington is, beyond all question, the first man, intellectually and morally, which this country has produced ; and of this, when you have made all allowance for the charming lustre with which time and history crown great characters, I think there can be no doubt. But his was not a character in which peculiarities shone pre-eminently : it was a character so well rounded, so controlled by the highest wisdom, that under all circumstances, and in every exigency of his private life, and in the administration of public affairs, he was able to do that, which, when revised by the sober judgment of the people, and subjected to the severest criticism, seems to have been the best thing under the circumstances. It is in the nature of things that men not so highly endowed in every direction are able to accomplish great results upon particular occasions ; indeed, there are times when men, by accident or by the force of circumstances, achieve what seems to be a great result in a particular case : but when, through a long period of years, and in all the various conditions of life, under circumstances which oftentimes have apparently the force of exigency, a man is able to so conduct himself as to stand the test of the judgment of the present and the future, there can no longer be a question as to the greatness of his faculties, or completeness of his powers. And such was Washington. As we close the first century of our national life, and attempt to penetrate the future, or at least to consider whether there is more which encourages hope or excites apprehension, I am glad to be able to say for myself, after considerable experience in public affairs and some knowledge of the people of my native State and of the country, that I am neither too timid nor too desponding to look with hope upon the future, and without serious apprehensions as to the character which this country is destined to have, either when tested by the individual men who compose and control it, or by the capacity of the people as a whole, or through their servants whom they may select to give guidance and control to public affairs, and which shall enable those who stand here a century hence to look with as much satisfaction upon the century which we now open as we now look upon the century which has just closed. That there have been, and that there always will be, in the management of public affairs, great errors, much to criticise, and much to condemn, is a truth incident to human existence. Errors are to be regretted, and their effects should be removed as far and as fast as possible: but he must be a misanthrope who looks only upon errors; who sees only the dark side of the picture; who sees only the clouds, and cannot imagine or believe that they have a silver lining. I say this here and now, because I think it of the highest importance that the young men of the country, especially those who have advantages of wealth, and opportunities for education, should see and feel, as I believe, that, in an attempt to discharge public duties through the acceptance of public office, they can maintain their integrity; that they can preserve their self-respect; and that they can pass through the fires and temptations of public life without the smell of the smoke of corruption upon their garments. If this be not so, then, indeed, the prospect for the future is dark, and I may say it is nearly hopeless. But it is not so. The recent dead testify that it is not so. Lincoln and Stanton and Sumner, from their graves and by their lives, bear witness that it is not so. And I wish to say to the young men who are entering upon the theatre of action, and have an opportunity to choose the way in which they will go, Look at the lives and the records of these men, imitate their example, and not be deterred by instances of a different character, which we desire to blot from the page of history and the memory of men: and though public duties when understood, and the responsibilities which they carry with them, are not attractive, there still is no way in which a young man of capacity and integrity can perform so signal service to his age and race as by accepting such opportunities as may be presented to him for the performance of those duties; and the opportunity to make laws, to frame, modify, or found institutions, is the greatest of human pursuits. Measured by any other merely secular standard, such labors rise high above every thing which concerns the fortunes of men in this world. Mr. Mayor, these remarks are not directly in response to the sentiment which preceded the announcement of my name; but if I have spoken at all in the interest of good government, in the interest of intelligence, and integrity in the management of public affairs, then I have said something in behalf of the United States. The United States are more closely united now than ever before. Every nation has a civilization in which there is a unit; otherwise it cannot last. Our nation, for nearly three-quarters of a century, moved in two directions, under the force of opposite ideas tending to different forms of civilization. To-day a deeper, stronger, more-pervading, better security for the future than are the opinions we entertain, or the hopes we cherished, is found in the fact that hereafter there is a unit in the civilization of this country: and a unit in the civilization of a country secures unity in the government. Therefore, while the civilization shall be a unit, the government will be a unit; and this government to-day rests upon two great ideas, — public equality and public education. When I reflect, as I do with gratitude and pride, that from the halls of this college, and from those of William and Mary's College in Virginia, went forth the men who embodied in their lives the doctrines and principles of the Revolution, I have faith in the schools, in the institutions of learning, and in the education of the people; and, having faith in schools and institutions of learning, I trust that we, and those who come after us, will adopt the language of our own Constitution and the language of the Father of his Country, on the walls of the college to-day, and that it will be the guide of our conduct in private and public affairs.

MUSIC BY THE BAND, — "America."

3. "*The Commonwealth of Massachusetts.*"

RESPONSE BY HIS EXCELLENCY GOVERNOR WILLIAM GASTON.

MR. MAYOR, LADIES AND GENTLEMEN, — The city of Cambridge certainly has much to be proud of. Her great institution of learning has for more than two centuries been sending forth to the world men who have been distinguished in science and in letters. It has furnished men who have made our history from the foundations of our State and Republic, — men who have carried the banners and blessings of a Christian civilization from ocean to ocean; and from her own citizens Cambridge has furnished men who have been distinguished as scholars, soldiers, and statesmen. Indeed, I know of no one place in the country which has furnished so many men who have been leaders in the cause of religion, morals, science, and patriotism. To-day she celebrates the coming within her borders of the great leader of the American army of the Revolution, — a man upon whom the language of eulogy has been exhausted.

His fame is sure, and he needs not the aid of our lips; but we, by admiring and contemplating his character, may become wiser, stronger, and better. Such I understand to be the meaning of this celebration: and such a purpose needs no commendation; for it carries with it its own justification, and even eulogy. And even at this time, when there is an opportunity for making our Federal Union more compact and united than ever, it is well, by celebrations like these, to contemplate the actions of men of preceding generations, in whose glory and fame all sections of the country have a common interest and pride. Then the celebration ceases to be a pageant, and is full of significance and meaning. I express much for old Cambridge when I hope that she will give to the future as much as she has given to the past. A hundred years ago, a Virginian came to Massachusetts: he came as the leader of our armies. The man and the event were alike majestic. He was welcomed to Massachusetts. Massachusetts and Virginia were then friends. I trust that kindred feelings exist to-day. But neither Massachusetts nor Virginia, neither North nor South, are worthy of him and his fame, unless they determine to preserve those institutions which he did so much to create.

MUSIC, — "Sweet Home."

4. *"The Old Thirteen."*

RESPONSE BY HON. JOSIAH QUINCY, OF BOSTON.

MR. CHAIRMAN, — It is almost impossible for the citizens of a republic whose domain extends from the Atlantic to the Pacific sea to realize the small extent and sparse population of the thirteen colonies, when, a hundred years ago, Washington drew his sword on the plain of Cambridge. Albany was almost a frontier-town, the Six Nations still existing on the Mohawk. The Monongahela and the Ohio, with the vast regions beyond, now the seats of noble cities and a dense population, were occupied by savages of different tribes. It is equally difficult for us to realize the position of Washington. The sparse population of the colonies were untrained to arms; they were separated by great distances, and wanted what Milton calls the "two main nerves of war, — iron and gold." The dark, impenetrable future loomed before him. By drawing that sword, he committed himself to the cause. The result might be victory, or it might be a soldier's death in battle, or a traitor's death on the scaffold. Besides a consciousness of duty, he had but one support. The plains of Lexington and Concord, and, but a few days before, the heights of Bunker, had given assurance that there were brave men, who were willing to serve with him, to fight with him, and, if need were, to die with him, for the liberty of their country. Such was his position on that day; but he was destined to receive aid and comfort from a most unexpected source.

In the gayest court of Europe there was a young nobleman of the highest rank and of ample fortune. He had just been united to one of the fairest daughters of France, who, in subsequent trials, proved that the strength of her mind corresponded with the loveliness of her person. With the chivalric spirit of his race, this young man espoused the cause of the weaker party. How weak that party was he well knew. In the language of Edward Everett (by which, in his presence fifty years ago, an audience was electrified, a few steps from where we stand), " When he applied to our commissioners in Paris for a passage in the first ship they should despatch to America, they were obliged to tell him, so poor and abject was then our dear native land, that they did not possess the means or the credit to procure a vessel in all the ports of France. 'Then,' exclaimed the youthful hero, 'I will procure my own.' And it is a literal fact, that when all America was too poor to give him even a passage to our shores, he left, in his tender youth, the bosom of home, of domestic happiness, of wealth and rank, to plunge into the dust and blood of our inauspicious struggle."

To the great majority of my hearers General Lafayette is only an historical character; and perhaps I cannot occupy the few moments allotted to me more agreeably or appropriately than in recalling some of the incidents connected with his visit fifty years ago. As aide to Governor Lincoln, I had the most favorable opportunity to witness the ceremonies connected with laying the corner-stone of Bunkerhill Monument, which, as you all remember, were honored by Lafayette's presence.

The 17th of June, 1825, dawned with uncommon splendor. The State of Massachusetts had voted a sum sufficient to pay the expenses of every soldier of the Revolution who reported himself on that day; and almost every survivor of that venerable band who resided in New England had availed himself of her bounty. From my official relations, I witnessed the meeting of these veterans. They had parted nearly half a century before. Their subsequent lot in life, or even their continued existence, had been to each other unknown. They met and recognized one another with almost the feelings of boys. The recollections of the past pressed upon their memories; and the flame of life, that had become almost extinguished in their bosoms, flashed out with its early brightness before it expired. It is an historical fact, that, when Washington decided to storm the two redoubts that enfiladed the approaches to Yorktown, he detailed two storming-parties, the one composed of Frenchmen and the other of Americans, and gave the command of the latter to Lafayette as a general in the American service. One of the veterans, when he was introduced, asked the general if he did not remember him; and added, "I was next but one to you when you mounted the ramparts at Yorktown. Sergeant Smith, who was between us, received a musket-ball in his head, and fell just as we mounted."—"I remember the circumstance perfectly," responded the general. "Poor Sergeant Smith! poor Sergeant Smith! But then," he added, with an eye gleaming with its earlier spirit, "*we got into the fort first: we beat the Frenchmen, my boy; we beat the Frenchmen!*" Such incidents were like removing the ashes that covered the spark of that love of liberty and military zeal that once set this continent in a flame. Forty years before, the patriot souls of these veterans scorned the advice not to disband until the nation had paid them for the services they had rendered; and they had left the army poor, and, from their military habits, unfitted to prosper in the civil occupations of life. Many of them had dragged on a despised and miserable existence, almost paupers in the land they had redeemed. The visit of Lafayette, and the recognition through him, and with him, of their services, was to them like the breaking-out of the setting sun after a day of storms, revealing the beauty of the land for which they had suffered, and giving them an assurance of its brighter to-morrow.

The masonic and military show had then never been surpassed; but the great interest of the scene arose from the presence of the survivors of the army of the Revolution. Of these, two hundred officers and soldiers led the way, and forty who had fought on Bunker's Hill followed in carriages. Lafayette was the only staff-officer of that venerable band that survived; and seven captains, three lieutenants, and one ensign, were all the other officers that remained.

After laying the corner-stone in due masonic order, Mr. Webster arose. He was then in the perfection of his manly beauty, fully realizing Milton's description of a superhuman statesman: —

> "With grave
> Aspect he rose, and in his rising seemed
> A pillar of state: deep on his front engraven
> Deliberation sat, and public care;
> And princely counsel in his face yet shone,
> Majestic. . . . Sage he stood,
> With Atlantean shoulders fit to bear
> The weight of mightiest monarchies: his look
> Drew audience and attention still as night,
> Or summer's noontide air, while thus he spoke."

No printed page, no effort of the pencil, could convey any adequate idea of the effect of his eloquence, or the scene that witnessed it, — the uncounted multitude; the distant city; the ocean beyond; the "oak leviathans" anchored at its base; the presence of those who fifty years before stood where they then stood, with their brothers and neighbors, shoulder to shoulder in strife for their country; and, above all, of him, who, connected with both hemispheres and two generations, had conducted the electric spark of liberty from the New World to the Old. As the orator carried us on from the glories of the past and the duties of the present to the destinies of the future, he enlarged our conceptions, and extended our ideas over the whole vast field in which we were called to act "to our country, our whole country, and nothing but our country."

But there was one exercise that by association filled the mind even more than the eloquence of Daniel Webster. The occasion was, of course, to be sanctified by prayer; and the venerable Joseph Thaxter, chaplain to Prescott's own regiment, rose to officiate. Fifty years before, he had stood upon that spot, and, in the presence of many for whom that morning sun was to know no setting, called on Him who could save by many or by few for his aid in the approaching struggle. His presence brought the scene vividly to our view. We could almost hear the thunder of the broadsides that ushered in that eventful morning. We could almost see Prescott and Warren and their gallant host pausing from their labors to listen to an invocation to Him before whom many ere nightfall were to appear. We could almost realize the anxieties that must have filled the minds of patriots before that first decisive conflict. Every thing else had changed: nothing remained the same but the Being before whom we bowed. He alone was the same, yesterday, to-day, and for ever.

After the ceremonies on Bunker's Hill, I had the privilege of attending General Lafayette through Massachusetts; and, occupying the same carriage, I had opportunities for long and most interesting conversations. His memory of past transactions was perfect; and he seemed to take a most benevolent pleasure in gratifying my curiosity by describing scenes through which he had passed, and the distinguished men and women with whom he had been associated. It was impossible to realize that the quiet and elegant gentleman at my side could have been the one who in the times of the French Revolution rode upon the storm, and, by kissing her hand, saved the beautiful Queen of France from an infuriated mob. Time forbids me to recount the amusing and interesting incidents connected with that journey.

Shortly after that visit, Lafayette returned to France to take a conspicuous part in the revolution that placed Louis Philippe on the throne. When last in Paris, I made a pilgrimage to his tomb. He lies in the cemetery of Picpus, which is connected with the garden of a nunnery belonging to the Sisters of the Sacred Heart. As you enter from the street under the massive stone gateway, you seem to have gone back for centuries. The whole appearance of the building and the grounds impress you with their extreme antiquity. It seems like a little eddy that revolves slowly in a narrow circle, while the great stream of time rushes rapidly by. We entered the chapel of the convent: on both sides of the altar were kneeling nuns, who were relieved as regularly as soldiers. This has continued for centuries. The storms of war or the earthquake of revolution may have convulsed the rest of the metropolis; but before this altar, by day and by night, without cessation, prayers have been offered for the happiness of the living and for the souls of the departed. I passed through the lofty walls that enclose the garden, and, at the end, was ushered into the cemetery. It is the resting-place of the old aristocracy of France. Every tomb is covered by a marble slab, and every one bears some historic name. At the extremity, one has this inscription: —

"HERE LIES GILBERT MOTIER LAFAYETTE,
LIEUTENANT-GENERAL AND DEPUTY.
BORN AT AUVERGNE A.D. 1757;
MARRIED MADE· NOAILLES 1776;
DIED 1834.
MAY HE REST IN PEACE."

It bears no record that he ever visited America. Twenty years ago, at a meeting of Americans in the city of Rome held in honor of the birthday of the father of our country, I mentioned the fact that no monument had ever been erected in honor of his friend and adopted son. A resolution was passed, and a subscription commenced, to erect an equestrian statue to the friend of America in the city of Paris. On application, however, through our minister, to learn whether such a monument would be permitted, we received a reply in the negative. The name of Lafayette might have conjured up a spirit that would have shaken the throne of Napoleon. No statue, no inscription in brass or marble, records what Lafayette did for the freedom of America. But there is a monument whose base extends from the Atlantic to the Pacific sea, whose apex rises higher and higher as it marks the progress of liberty protected by law. On its sides are inscribed many names that shall be immortal; but, above all, most conspicuous are those of our NATION's FATHER and our NATION's FRIEND.

Music, — "Auld Lang Syne."

5. "*The Army and Navy of the United States.*"

RESPONSE BY GENERAL CHARLES DEVENS, JR.,
Of Worcester.

MR. MAYOR, — It is quite unexpected that I find myself here this afternoon; but it is as pleasant as it is unexpected. The only alloy to it is the fact that I am expected to stand up here three or four minutes and talk. A few moments ago I was requested to respond to a toast to the judiciary; and now it seems that the toast-master has called upon me to respond to a sentiment to the army and navy. I am too well acquainted with the authority which the toast-master of a feast is to exercise, and I am entirely willing to submit to his will, which is absolute as that of the captain upon the quarter-deck. I rise to cordially respond to the sentiment: certainly none could be more appropriate to the place where we stand; for it was here that the army and navy were created. I thank the corporation of the city of Cambridge that it has not allowed this great and important day to pass without due recognition, and that it has called us together in this place, which is so fragrant with Revolutionary reminiscences, to commune together. We are in the great historic county of Middlesex, — the historic county of Massachusetts, where the three great steps towards the independence of these States were made. At Lexington and Concord, Massachusetts was alone. There, alone, she lifted her lion head in the stern defence of liberty. At Bunker Hill, the States of New England had gathered by her side; and there all the colonies stood together in their resistance to British power. The third step came when the United Colonies of North America were represented here by the consolidation. by the act of the Continental Congress, of this army of New England into the Continental army, and by the occasion when Washington, as Commander-in-Chief, drew his sword under the tree around which we walked to-day. The sword that flashed in the sunlight represented the union of the colonies of North America. It is in this capacity that I love to remember him as representing the union of these States. From the moment he arrived, the army of Massachusetts, the army of New England, bravely and nobly as they had done, were merged in the Continental Army. Massachusetts, the great State of the Revolution, — I speak now by the record and the book, — which furnished to the Continental Army more than one-fourth of the men who fought in it, from that time consented to be a member of the Union, and that her soldiers should be led by officers who were appointed by the Continental Congress. As we progress with the review of the character of Washington, we see him everywhere associated with the union of the States. When the great war was done, when those years of anxiety and despondency succeeded, before a regular government could be formed, when we looked about in fear lest we were to become mere discordant States, when that great convention came together which made us a nation and a people, Washington was its president. When that Constitution went into operation, after the long debates that had followed, the president chosen under that Constitution to administer its civil powers was Washington; and the event that we celebrate to-day represents the union of these States as the United States. Grand and proud as we have the right to be here in Middlesex and Massachusetts as represented at Concord and Lexington, and in New England as represented at Bunker Hill, yet, when we have all come together under the great flag of a united people, we still have the right to be more proud that it was in our old county that this occurred. It was with great regret that I reached the tent where we held our exercises only at the conclusion of the address of the orator of the occasion. No nobler subject could be chosen than that which he selected, — " The Character of Washington." Surely there is no nobler subject for contemplation than the life of a truly great, truly brave, and honest man. When we speak of him, we seem to lift ourselves up into a calmer and serener atmosphere.

In that era of romance that preceded the coming of the Christian religion, — that world which was peopled with gods and goddesses, — it was fabled that the heroes were demi-gods. Raised above the race of man, and yet not so far but that their example might be imitated, they united man to the immortal gods themselves, "enthroned upon their sacred seats," and by their example sought to elevate him to a higher and nobler life. So to-day with us in the recollection of great, heroic lives; in the contemplation of great, heroic souls. Though the dust of the struggle is upon us as we stand mingling in the fierce conflict of the world's arena, by their example we are inspired to a higher and purer existence. When we remember at what a price this liberty was achieved, let us endeavor to render the homage which the orator of to-day has desired we should render to the men by whom it was achieved, by striving to imitate their patriotism and self-devotion. To the corruptions that seem always destined to come into the administration of great states, as the dry-rot eats into the strong oak-timbers of our mighty ships, let us show ourselves stern and implacable foes; to the luxury that enervates nations, let us oppose the simple dignity of manly and laborious toil in our respective spheres of duty; and let us stand together always in honest love and regard for all our fellow-citizens, no matter what their position may be, whether high or humble, — no matter what their race or color, or previous condition.

Music, — "The Red, White, and Blue."

6. "Harvard University."

RESPONSE BY CHARLES W. ELIOT,

President of Harvard University.

Mr. Mayor, Ladies and Gentlemen, — Harvard College bore its full share of the sacrifices which the Revolution demanded. Its income was reduced; its books and apparatus were scattered in private houses in Andover, Concord, and Woburn, for two years; and its buildings were seriously damaged by the troops who occupied them during the long investment of Boston. But whatever losses and hardships the college suffered during the Revolution were gladly borne; for then, as ever since, the College was heart and soul on the side of liberty. Its government was of the patriot party; its president was an outspoken advocate of popular rights; and many of the foremost leaders of the people were sons of the College. I need not extol these immortal sons of Harvard; for their names are household words wherever liberty is precious. The generations to come will look upon James Otis, John Hancock, Samuel Adams, John Adams, and Joseph Warren with all the admiration with which we regard them; for the world will not see purer patriots or braver men. Here they were nurtured; here they drank at the life-giving springs of piety, eloquence, and poetry; here they read of chivalry and freedom, and of the heroic days of Greece and Rome and England; here they breathed together, in their impressible youth, that spirit of liberty which characterized the place and the times.

Institutions of learning may always be counted upon the side of freedom; because literature, philosophy, and science confer distinction and power without respect of persons, with small regard to birth, wealth, or any privileges not based on mental or spiritual gifts; and because, too, they ameliorate the common lot, inspire the common mind, and tend to equalize conditions of life. Universities worthy of the name are always liberal in a true sense.

We commemorate the men of 1775, that we and our children may better emulate them. We have needed, and our children will need, their heroic virtues. The government which they founded has had a prodigious development, until it has become the grandest and most hopeful, but also the most awful and inscrutable, experiment in government ever made. Old-world people have often pictured to themselves the New World as a very paradise of freedom, peace, and plenty; but, if it has been a paradise at all, it has been a paradise, like Mahomet's, under the shadow of swords. Since the Jesuits first undertook to evangelize the savage continent, American history has been one long story of almost incessant fighting. The Spaniards fought with the French; the French with the Spaniards, the English, and the colonists; all these invaders with the Indians; the English with their colonists; the United States with England, with Mexico, and with the Indians; and finally the States waged terrible civil war among themselves. For several generations, our New-England people were martial to an extraordinary degree. Let us not forget that the greatest of Americans, Washington, was a professional soldier, and that we celebrate this day because on this spot he took command of a rude army, sprung from the soil on the night of Lexington, composed of men who thought liberty was to be fought for. Each succeeding century of American history has been bloodier than the preceding. What has been will be, until public wrongs are done no more, and the fierce passions of ungovernable multitudes can no more be kindled. Therefore we exalt the courage, ardor, and instinctive devotion which make the patriot soldier; therefore we praise his patience and fortitude amid hardships, his calm encounter with mortal danger, his quiet endurance even of neglect and ingratitude, his unquenchable loyalty to his flag and his country, without foresight of the issue, without knowing even whether his sacrifice will avail any thing for his country. These are great virtues, great and strong enough to bring good out of fearful evil.

Our forefathers had their perils and ills: our children will have theirs. With halters round their necks, with no organized government at their backs, a thick veil hanging over their future, our ancestors took their guns, and went out to kill as many Englishmen as they could. That seemed to them their nearest duty, and they did it. They could at least see well enough the whites of their enemies' eyes. What immeasurable consequences have flowed from their dauntless vindication of what they held to be their rights!

And now, a century after the bloody birth of the nation, new dangers and strange internal evils threaten. We must meet them as our fathers met their trials. We must find such leaders as they found; men of education, men of property, and men of honor. The men who signed the Declaration of Independence pledged to each other their lives, their fortunes, and their sacred honor. Their lives, of course, for they were contending with a power which had much experience in executing traitors and putting rebels to the sword; their fortunes, for confiscation was a weapon of both parties, and they put at risk not only their property, but also their prospects and their reputations, and their sacred honor. Those men had honor as well as fortunes to pledge.

We do well, then, to commemorate the patriots of the Revolution, that their example may strengthen our hearts, that our children may catch their spirit, and win the sturdy virtues which defy dangers and master evils.

Music, — "Fair Harvard."

7. *"The Grand Lodge of Massachusetts."*

RESPONSE BY MOST WORSHIPFUL GRAND MASTER
PERCIVAL L. EVERETT,

Of Boston.

MR. MAYOR, — The Society of Freemasonry feels a deep interest in every thing relating to the memory of Washington; for he in his lifetime was a friend and patron of our Society, and one of its most honored and revered members. The year after he was born, Freemasonry was established at Boston by the warrant of Viscount Montague, then Grand Master of England.

Benjamin Franklin, then residing at Philadelphia, derived his powers to establish the Society in Pennsylvania from Boston, and became Grand Master of that State. In 1752, at Fredericksburg, Va., George Washington, as the record now in existence attests, was initiated into the Fraternity, in a Lodge organized by the warrant of Thomas Oxnard of Boston, Provincial Grand Master.

In those early days of the Society's existence in America it had won the respect and regard of all good citizens. Governor Belcher was one of its prominent and influential members, and, both here and in the Province of New Jersey, exhibited publicly his attachment to the Fraternity.

In later days, among the patrons and strong supporters of our institution may be mentioned the names of John Warren, Joseph Webb, Josiah Bartlett, Timothy Bigelow, and John Dixwell, each of whom occupied the position of

Grand Master of Masons in Massachusetts; while among the Grand Chaplains there were Thaddeus Mason Harris, William Bentley, John Eliot, and Ezra Ripley. It may be interesting for me to mention, as showing the unsectarianness of Masonry, that our Grand Chaplains have been divided denominationally as follows: Unitarian, 20; Episcopalian, 16; Trinitarian Congregationalist, 9; Methodist Episcopal, 5; Baptist, 4; Christian Baptist, 1.

In the "History of Washington and his Masonic Compeers," Sidney Hayden says, in alluding to Peyton Randolph, "In 1773, committees of correspondence began to be formed in the different colonies to ascertain the true position and sentiments of each. Of that of Virginia, Mr. Randolph was chairman; and through him the Cavaliers of Virginia became first united in political sentiment with the Puritans of New England. We cannot attempt in this personal sketch of Mr. Randolph to give a portraiture of the events of those times, or of the influences that produced them: suffice it to say, that there is an unwritten history of the silent influences of Masonry in producing the political associations of that period. The mighty Brotherhood of Masonry, ever the friend of freedom, was omnipotent for good."

Here in Massachusetts, many of the leading spirits of the Revolution, such as Joseph Warren and Paul Revere, were presiding over our Grand Lodge. The history of the meetings at the Green-Dragon Tavern, and the influence of this society in bringing about and shaping the Revolution, have yet to be written. But that this influence was strong and controlling is beyond all question. How much Franklin accomplished through the Fraternity of France, in the lodges in which he received many an ovation, the world does not know.

After Washington became a member of the Ancient and Honorable Society of Freemasonry, he continued until his death to be its firm and devoted friend. The doings of the society have not been open to the public gaze; yet it is a fact worth considering, that, during all the eventful life of Washington, he was surrounded by members of this fraternity. Nearly all the General Officers of the Revolution were Masons. This was equally true of the members of the first Congress. Nearly all of the signers of the Declaration of Independence were active members of our Society; and the President of the first Continental Congress was Grand Master of Masons in Virginia.

How much the intimacy and close union of its members, and especially the confidence and reliance which this Society produced among the men of the Revolution in the field and in the senate, nerved their arms and increased their courage, we cannot tell; but we can believe, that, in the many hours of gloom and despondency which overshadowed the just cause before it finally prevailed, the friendships and strong hopes which were engendered by this confidence and reliance had much to do with the final result.

After the conflict was over, the Union was established, and Washington's fame was world-wide. — " first in war, first in peace, and first in the hearts of his countrymen,"— he did not consider it beneath his dignity to mix with the Fraternity, and be known as one of its members.

When the corner-stone of the national Capitol was laid, in the city named for the Father of his Country. Washington was present as a Freemason to testify to the world, that, however exalted his station, he was not ashamed to acknowledge his connection with the Order. He had many examples before him in the Old World, and many have followed in his footsteps; since the Grand Masters of England, for the last century and a half, have nearly all ranked high in the peerage. The heirs-apparent of England and Prussia preside over their respective Grand Lodges to-day, while kings and emperors have added to their numerous titles that of Grand Master of the Freemasons.

In the declining years of Washington's life, the Grand Lodge of Massachusetts received from him two communications in answer to congratulatory letters officially sent to him. These letters are well known to the Fraternity, and have frequently been published in their proceedings. It is not our fault that they are not equally well known to the public.

Suffice it to say, that, in these communications, he exhibits the same loyalty to this Order which had been conspicuous throughout his entire Masonic life.

When the sad end came, and all that was mortal of this illustrious man was left behind, his remains were deposited in the tomb by the loving hands of his Brethren, to whom he had always been faithful.

The Grand Lodge of Massachusetts communicated its grief to Mrs. Washington: and she, well knowing the high regard which Washington, living, had always entertained for Freemasonry, sent to our Grand Lodge this lock of his hair. [The lock of hair, in a golden urn, was here shown to the company.] The patriot Revere enclosed it, with his own hands, in this golden urn; and once a year, at the installation of all my predecessors, this urn, with its precious treasure, has been confided to the care and custody of the Grand Master of Masons in this Commonwealth.

Standing in the historic relation to Washington which the Grand Lodge of Massachusetts sustains, it is a source of pleasure and pious duty for us to join with you in this centennial celebration. Here he first assumed the command of the Continental forces; nor did he yield it until he had given freedom and liberty to his country, until he had established a nation in peace.

8. "*The Patriots of the Late War.*"

RESPONSE OF MAJOR GEORGE S. MERRILL,

Of Lawrence,

COMMANDER OF DEPARTMENT OF MASSACHUSETTS GRAND ARMY OF THE REPUBLIC.

MR. MAYOR, LADIES AND GENTLEMEN, — I am scarcely less embarrassed in this presence, and with these associations and surroundings, than by the realization of the utter insufficiency of any words of mine to answer for the men to whom your sentiment alludes. Indeed, sir, I am a little puzzled to know precisely why I was called upon to fill this position. It was not my good fortune to have been born in Cambridge, or even in Boston; although I hardly think I should blame myself for that: but possibly I may have discovered the reason in the suggestion of the President of Harvard University, that, during the stormy hours of the Revolution, a portion of the library of the college was preserved in Andover, from whose territory was taken a portion of the city in which I reside; and it is possible that the circulation of the contents of the library may account for the somewhat peculiar theology of that honored town. At all events, it is not impossible that a portion of the library still remaining there, its loss may have had some influence upon the theology of this ancient institution of yours. But, sir, I am thankful that the men to whom your sentiment alludes need no eulogy from human lips. From the days of 1861 to those of 1865, from Baltimore to New Orleans, from the Atlantic to the Mississippi, from Atlanta to the ocean, on more than a hundred battle-fields by land and by sea, they spoke for themselves. And to-day, at the close of the first decade since Peace shed its shining beams through the length and breadth of our broad land, standing upon the threshold of the second century, these soldiers of the Republic, while relinquishing none of the principles for which they suffered, still speak, by heart and hand and voice, only for peace, unity, and reconciliation. The events of the Revolution and of the Rebellion are more closely united than we are wont to think. The tie that binds the events of 1775 to those of 1861 must not be measured by the span of years. No nation of the past has preserved the story of its heroes more carefully than has been handed down to us, from sire to son, the treasured memories of a hundred years ago. That this story has not been without its beneficial results, we have but to remember that it was the men of Middlesex, who, when the red torch of war was lighted in our land, first rallied beneath the old flag in defence of the liberties of the Union, and that the blood of Massachusetts was first drank in by the soil of Maryland. And surely, during all the long years of the war, there were no more chivalrous soldiers following the flag, no more patriotic blood was shed in defence of national unity and national integrity, no purer lives were laid upon the altar of the country, than came from the honored walls of Harvard and the classic soil of Cambridge. And as we in Massachusetts join in these centennials, — fortunate, as has been said, that we have within our limits so many of these memorable spots, — and as we have already seen uncounted thousands coming, not to witness the pageant of a great show, but, with pure love in their hearts for the memories of their fathers, on a pilgrimage to the graves of those early martyrs upon which rests the silence of a century; and later have seen nearly half a million of our people join in celebrating the anniversary of that great event, the battle of Bunker Hill, witnessed the waving of handkerchiefs, and shouting of huzzas, to the men who stood in opposition to our own soldiers in the South, in token of appreciation of the better days of peace that have come upon us; and as we come now to this still greater anniversary, of the day when the town-meeting — if we may so term it — of the early Colonies became a consolidated army, and, through the genius of the commander-in-chief, accomplished that most unparalleled act in history, — the driving of the English army from the soil they had once fully possessed, — while we now look forward across the threshold of the opening century, and gather up the eternal glories of the years gone by, be it ours to so live and act in the present, that, when our sons shall join in the next grand centennial, they may repeat the names of this generation as kindly, and treasure our memories as tenderly, as do we to-day those of the early patriots and soldiers upon whose deeds has already fallen the misty mantle of a century.

Music, — "Hail Columbia."

9. "*The Orator of the Day.*"

RESPONSE BY REV. A. P. PEABODY, D.D.,

Of Cambridge, the Orator of the Day.

MR. MAYOR, — It is better not to try a hazardous experiment twice. I have, to be sure, once exercised self-denial to the last degree: and certainly the self-denial was fully equal to your patience; for, if I had told you one-half of what I have talked and felt in my preparation for this day, your dinner would have remained uneaten till the present moment. I am not going to inflict upon you what I did not say then; but let me say, that we, here in Cambridge and in Harvard College, are doing all in our power to keep the succession of patriotic citizens. I will say for my colleagues in office, that one of our chief cares is to give our students a profound sense of their responsibility to the State which nurtures them, to the country whose citizens they are to become; and I believe that, from year to year, we are sending out our full quota of men who will be worthy pillars of the State, and, I am glad to add, worthy pillars of the Church.

10. "*The Poet of the Day.*"

RESPONSE BY PROF. JAMES RUSSELL LOWELL,

Of Cambridge, the Poet of the Day.

MR. MAYOR, LADIES AND GENTLEMEN, — I was obliged, by my official position last Wednesday at the Harvard Alumni meeting, to make so many speeches in this hall, that I seem to see an expression of astonishment on the faces of the portraits opposite, as if to say, "What! is he up again?" But I had my shot at you three or four hours ago; and I don't intend to make use of the privilege the toast-master has given me, except in the sense that it is understood to have been given, — that is, it is not a toast to the poet of the occasion, but to the poets of Cambridge; and I officiate only for the purpose of introducing my friend Dr. HOLMES, who will respond to the spirit of the toast.

RESPONSE BY DR. OLIVER WENDELL HOLMES,

Of Boston.

LADIES AND GENTLEMEN, — I know you will not accuse me of lightly or wantonly taking the compliment to myself, when you have sat to-day and listened to my friend's inspiring poem; and I should hesitate to read the few verses I have here, were it not that one was before and the other after dinner. I have addressed the gray heads and bald heads of this assembly more particularly, asking if they can tell where some of the old familiar places in this immediate vicinity are.

    AND can it be you've found a place
    Within this consecrated space,
        Which makes so fine a show,
    For one of Rip Van Winkle's race?
        And is it really so?
    Who wants an old, receipted bill?
    Who fishes in the Frog-pond still?
    Who digs last year's potato-hill?
        That's what he'd like to know!

    And were it any spot on earth
    Save this dear home that gave him birth
        Some scores of years ago,
    He had not come to spoil your mirth
        And chill your festive glow;
    But round his baby-nest he strays,
    With tearful eye the scene surveys,
    His heart unchanged by changing days;
        That's what he'd have you know.

    Can you whose eyes not yet are dim
    Live o'er the buried past with him,
        And see the roses blow
    When white-haired men were Joe and Jim,
        Untouched by winter's snow?

Or roll the years back one by one,
As Judah's monarch backed the sun,
 And see the century just begun?
  That's what he'd like to know!

I came but as the swallow dips,
Just touching with her feather-tips
 The shining wave below,
To sit with pleasure-murmuring lips,
 And listen to the flow
Of Elmwood's sparkling Hippocrene, —
To tread once more my native green,
To sigh unheard, to smile unseen, —
  That's what I'd have you know.

But since the common lot I've shared
(We all are sitting "unprepared"
 Like culprits in a row,
Whose heads are down, whose necks are bared
 To wait the headsman's blow),
I'd like to shift my task to you,
By asking just a thing or two
About the good old times I knew:
  Here's what I want to know:

The yellow meet'n'-house — can you tell
Just where it stood before it fell
 Prey of the levelling foe? —
Our dear old temple, loved so well,
 By ruthless hands laid low.
Where, tell me, was the Deacon's pew?
Whose hair was braided in a queue?
(For there were pig-tails not a few) —
  That's what I'd like to know.

The bell — can you recall its clang?
And how the seats would slam and bang?
 The viol and its bow?
The basso's trump before he sang?
 And sweet voiced Nat. Munroe?
Where was it old Judge Winthrop sat?
Who wore the last three-cornered hat?
Was Israel Porter lean or fat?
  That's what I'd like to know.

Tell where the market used to be
That stood beside the murdered tree?
    Whose dog to church would go?
Old Marcus Reemie, who was he?
    Who were the brothers Snow?
Does not your memory slightly fail
About that great September gale
Whereof one told a moving tale
    As Cambridge boys should know?

When Cambridge was a simple town
Say just where Deacon William Brown
    (Look round in yonder row)
For honest silver counted down
    His groceries would bestow? —
For those were days when money meant
Something that jingled as you went, —
No hybrid like the nickel cent,
    I'd have you all to know;

But quarter, ninepence, pistareen,
And fourpence ha'pennies in between,
    All metal fit to show,
Instead of rags in stagnant green,
    The scum of debts we owe.
How sad to think such stuff should be
Our Wendell's cure-all remedy; —
Not Wendell II., but Wendell P., —
    The one you all must know!

I question — but you answer not —
Dear me! and have I quite forgot
    How five-score years ago,
Just on this very blessed spot,
    The summer leaves below,
Before his homespun ranks arrayed,
In green New England's elm-bough shade
The great Virginian drew the blade
    King George full soon should know!

O George the Third! you found it true
Our George was more than double you,

> For nature made him so.
> Not much a jewelled cap can do
> If brains are scant and slow.
> Ah, not like that his laurel crown
> Whose presence gilded with renown
> Our brave old Academic town,
> As all her children know!
>
> To-day we meet with loud acclaim
> To tell mankind that here he came,
> With hearts that throb and glow;
> Ours is a portion of his fame,
> Our trumpets needs must blow!
> On yonder hill the Lion fell,
> But here was chipped the Eagle's shell, —
> That little hatchet did it well,
> We mean the world shall know!

11. "1775 — *Massachusetts* — 1875."

RESPONSE BY HON. EMORY WASHBURN,

Of Cambridge, Ex-Governor of Massachusetts.

MR. MAYOR, LADIES AND GENTLEMEN, — You have put me in a worse situation than were any of the soldiers who stood on the Common when General Washington drew his sword. They were without guns and ammunition; and so am I. But they were volunteers; and I am not. I came without any gun or ammunition, and without the slightest intimation that I would be expected to fire off any thing here to-day; and yet you call upon me to speak for Massachusetts, and for 1775 as compared with 1875. Mr. Mayor, if you expect me to give a history of what has transpired in Massachusetts since 1775, you ought to have begun earlier in the afternoon; for I have hardly time: besides, my friends who have gone before me have taken up all the events. But, sir, if you wish to compare the spirit of to-day with the spirit of 1775, and wish me, from the reminiscences that I have of local history, to present before this audience some examples of what indi-

cated the spirit of 1775, you will pardon me, sir, if I go
back in those recollections to the incidents in a single town,
in order to illustrate what I have to say. I speak, sir, of a
town some fifty miles from this place: and my object in
reverting to it is to show the state of feeling that then prevailed in Massachusetts; the universal feeling among every
class in the community; the readiness with which, when
the war came, they met it, although they were destitute of
the means that would enable them to encounter the then most
glorious and powerful nation upon earth. I speak of an
incident connected with one town which I know to be true.
On the 19th of April, 1775, at a little past twelve o'clock
noon, a messenger arrived in that town, giving information
to the commander of a volunteer company which had been
organized there, but whose members were spread over a
territory six miles square. Riding up to a shop, the messenger said to the man, "The war has begun!—the
British are marching on Concord!" Then on he went
to alarm the towns in the west. This was fifty miles from
Boston, and a little after twelve o'clock noon. Who sent him,
nobody knew; what authority he had, nobody knows. They
didn't ask what his authority was. There were only a
hundred and fifty men on the roll of soldiers of the town;
but in less than four hours, fifty of those men had been
gathered together from the six square miles of that town,
coming as they did from their ploughs in the fields and from
their shops, and crossing fields and woods to reach the
rendezvous. Before five o'clock they had been mustered
on the Common, their minister had offered up prayer,—
for they were a praying as well as a patriotic people,—and
they were on the march for Concord. There wasn't a house
but was lighted to encourage the soldiers on their way. At
Marlboro', they found that the British had gone back into
Boston. It was no idle talk; they came ready for action;
and, when Washington took command here, that company
was in the line. There wasn't a man of them but had some
war-mark upon his person or clothing; for they had been

through the fire of the battle of Bunker Hill; and the captain who stood there had four bullets through the cloak he wore upon that occasion. That, sir, was a mere representative of the Massachusetts men who came to stand by what they had heard preached, and were willing to practise. Now, sir, the question comes up, Is the spirit that animated those men the same spirit that animates us to-day? What are the changes that have come over Massachusetts? Why, sir, in material prosperity, there is no comparison between the condition of the country then and what it is now. Massachusetts was a beggar, comparatively, then: her resources were gone. When that company marched by the last house in their town, the mother of one of the soldiers came out to bid her son good-bye; and she asked the captain if he had any ammunition. He said he had powder, but no bullets. She said, "Wait a few moments," and went into the house. Taking the weights from the old family clock, she melted them up, holding them over the fire herself. That was a sample of the spirit that pervaded Massachusetts then. But, sir, Massachusetts has changed since then. In material prosperity there is no comparison. We now have two thousand millions of dollars of valuation; but have we the same spirit that we had then? Are we as rich in the spirit of manliness, justice, and confidence in God, that characterized the men of New England and Massachusetts who gathered here upon this plain when Washington took command? Sir, before these centennial anniversaries began, I had thought that our patriotism was almost dying out; and it almost seemed that another century would wind up the history of Massachusetts and the United States as that of the Rome of old had been wound up; that corruption in party politics and party leaders would poison the very foundation of the government under which we live. But when I have heard the speeches made here to-day, and felt the spirit with which you have come to these successive anniversaries, when I have noticed the ready responses to the eloquent and patriotic appeals of our orator and poet, I have been convinced that the hearts of the people are right, and that the people are as true now as they were then. And when I see that our institutions of learning have improved with the growth of our national prosperity, remembering that this hall is to be the representative of the advance that has been made in Harvard College since the soldiers took possession of it a century ago, I feel my confidence renewed, that, when another century comes round, Massachusetts will be found where she was in 1775, and where she is now; that the United States will be found where they are now; and that we shall not have become corrupt enough to lose our government, or forfeit our freedom. Why, sir, every thing encourages us. See what has been accomplished in the last century! We once talked of the dissolution of the Union, and the danger of the government being broken to pieces; but haven't we got rid of the great cause of dissatisfaction and disagreement between the two sections of the country? And when the centennial came round, and we went upon Bunker Hill to renew our vows to the country, and to the cause for which our fathers fought, bled, and died, did we not there meet our brethren from the South, and pledge each other that the Union should be for all time? When I see this spirit, I don't care if there be corruption in some of our party leaders; I don't care if our rulers are at times defective: I do not fear, for I know that we have the same spirit which actuated the common people of Massachusetts in 1775, and that in 1975 they will be ready to celebrate, as we do now, the union, freedom, and independence of our country; and that the United States then will stand, not merely as a single republic among the monarchies of the Old World, but the leading power among the republics of free States throughout the world.

   Music, — "The Star-Spangled Banner."

12. "*Lexington, Concord, and Bunker Hill.*"

RESPONSE BY HON. GEO. WASHINGTON WARREN.

<small>Of Boston, on behalf of the Bunker-Hill-Monument Association.</small>

MR. MAYOR, — It is quite a task for one person to speak for those three names, when each has had an orator and a poet, within the last few weeks to illustrate it. The eloquence of Dana, Curtis, and Devens has clothed those immortal names with a new lustre. And as to the great name we have *here* assembled to commemorate, — where occurred the third great act in the cause of the nation, — we all know that it is not only respected here, but in every part of the world. Many years ago, I happened to have an instance of it come home to myself. While travelling on the continent of Europe, I found, that, in presenting my passport, I was received with the greatest politeness and most profound respect; and the same was the case with a company of ladies who were with me. We frequently spoke of the politeness of the officers. It was marked in the cities of Italy, where the idea prevails that one cannot take the name of another unless he belongs to the family. So far as I am concerned, they were right: for Washington was the Father of his Country, and any citizen of the United States has the right to bestow that name upon his progeny; and I am only one of a thousand bearing that name. Mr. Mayor, I think this festive gathering at the close of these ceremonies is very appropriately held in this building, erected as it was in honor of those who preserved the country which Washington came here to defend; and it is also appropriate because of the peculiar relation which the college has held to this ancient town. Why, sir, the American army graduated here in the first place; and when the memorable expedition was formed, and when Prescott formed his regiment into a hollow square, he received a blessing from the lips of the President of Harvard College. If the present President of the College were a clerical man, he would certainly have been called upon to perform the service of chaplain on Bunker Hill at the last anniversary: in 1857, when the statue of General Warren was inaugurated, the then President of Harvard College acted in that capacity. I give you, sir, as a sentiment, —

All honor to the city of Cambridge, which is the birth-place of American scholarship, and is also the birth-place of the Union army which gave us a nation for that scholarship to lead and adorn.

13. "*Our Centennial.*"

RESPONSE BY GEN. EDWARD W. HINCKS, U.S.A.,

Of Milwaukee, Wis. (formerly resident in Cambridge).

MR. MAYOR, — When my friend General Devens responded for the army and navy, I supposed that I had escaped further service upon this occasion; but he suggested that it perhaps had been reserved for me to speak for the judiciary! Now I find myself called upon to respond to the toast of the day which, when given in this hall, should have commanded the eloquence of a gifted son of Harvard. We have to-day been reminded by learned speakers that this nation was born of the sword; and the record of its growth tells us that, in every epoch of its history, the tree of Liberty has been nurtured by the blood of the slain. Yet we cannot forget, that, in the progress of these hundred years just passed, the greatest triumphs won by our countrymen have been attained in peaceful industries, and in the walks of law, literature, and the arts. As we contemplate with so much satisfaction the bright record of our nation in the first century of its age, and hope with so much confidence for grander achievements during the century upon which we are about to enter, may we not appropriately avail ourselves of the opportunity afforded by these centennial festivities to cast the mantle of charity over all the acts of our fellow-citizens who have differed with us in years recently passed? Surely they were our countrymen, however misguided; theirs was the valor of America's sons contending for what they believed to be the right. The record of their heroic devotion, and of the virtues of their great military chieftain, is the legacy of the whole American people, as much so as is the imperishable fame of him whose deeds have been commemorated to-day, or the heroic names inscribed upon the marble tablets within this hall. The most gratifying indications of the times are the evidences, multiplying on every hand, that the birth of the new century is to be marked by an era of national fellowship and good-will, — without which the Union would be but a pillar of sand; that the enmities and estrangements engendered in all our conflicts are to be forgotten, and that the whole American people are again to be resolved into one harmonious brotherhood, having mutual sympathies and interests, cherishing one love of country, actuated by one desire to uphold the laws, and governed by one impulse of patriotism, manliness, and honesty; — an era in which our country shall return to the path of its true grandeur, and renew its marvellous career, leading in the march of a purer civilization, and winning the bloodless victories of perpetual peace.

THE CHILDREN'S ENTERTAINMENT.

ONE of the most pleasing features of the 3d of July celebration was the children's entertainment in the afternoon.

While the dinner was in progress at Memorial Hall, about twenty-five hundred children assembled in the tent, with their parents and teachers surrounding them, closely packed to the extreme verge, and fringed beyond by an encircling band of patient listeners.

The exercises were under the direction of the energetic projector of the entertainment, Mr. BENJAMIN WOODWARD; assisted by Mr. CHARLES E. BOYD as musical director (he having also conducted the previous rehearsals), with Mr. CHARLES STIMPSON as aid. The large number taking part made the active and faithful services of Mr. J. EDWIN MULLEN, as secretary, well worthy of notice.

The musical part of the programme was furnished by thirty-seven young ladies, and an equal number of young gentlemen, representing the thirty-seven States of the Union, assisted by an extra chorus of eight voices; Mrs. E. F. BOWKER, soprano, and Mr. JOSEPH CLAUS, baritone, soloists; Mr. L. L. POWERS, pianist; and EDMANDS' ORCHESTRA.

Shortly after four o'clock, the curtain which concealed the platform was withdrawn, and a beautiful tableau was presented, which called forth unbounded applause: the chorus being arranged in the form of an eagle with widespread wings, and the Goddess of Liberty as the head; the latter being personated by Miss BELLE GRIEVES.

The thirteen original States were represented as follows; the young ladies being dressed in white with designative sashes, and the young gentlemen wearing the Continental hat and an appropriate regalia: —

Virginia . . .	Miss KITTY M. SHAW.	Mr. EDWARD BROOKS.
New York . .	„ GEORGIANNA JONES.	„ FRANK HOWLETT.
Massachusetts .	„ MAY SHEPHERD.	„ FREDERICK HOWE.
New Hampshire	„ ANNIE SPROULE.	„ J. EDW. MULLEN.
Connecticut . .	„ NELLIE L. PIKE.	„ J. EDW. GRIEVES.
Maryland . . .	„ CARRIE BURTON.	„ WM. WORCESTER.
Rhode Island .	„ MARIA M. HILLMAN.	„ CHARLES GRIEVES.
Delaware . . .	„ ELLA F. LENFEST.	„ MARTIN P. BEARCE.
North Carolina .	„ FLOR. RICHARDSON.	„ JOHN A. BARRY.
New Jersey . .	„ LILLIAS D. BOYD.	„ FRANK C. DENNIS.
South Carolina .	„ EUDORA WARD.	„ EDWARD F. FORBES.
Pennsylvania .	„ ELLA R. GRIEVES.	„ GEO. H. MUNROE.
Georgia . . .	„ LIZZIE BURTON.	„ WM. M. GORDON.

The other States were represented as follows; the young ladies being dressed in white with designative sashes, and the young gentlemen wearing the full Continental uniform: —

Vermont . . .	Miss ALICE LLOYD.	Mr. EDWARD DOWNING.
Kentucky . . .	„ AGNES M. BOYD.	„ JOHN GIBSON.
Tennessee . .	„ MABEL HOOKER.	„ GEORGE H. NIXON.
Ohio	„ IDA MUMLER.	„ CHARLES ALDEN.
Louisiana . . .	„ MAGGIE WILLIAMS.	„ ROBERT MALCOLM.
Indiana . . .	„ JESSIE L. HALLENBECK.	„ GEORGE E. BROWN.
Mississippi . .	„ NELLIE LONGLEY.	„ EDW. H. MORRISON.
Illinois	„ MARY HARRINGTON.	„ JOHN HARRINGTON.
Alabama . . .	„ MAGGIE BRYANT.	„ FREDERICK ALLEN.
Maine	„ CARRIE A. SMITH.	„ EDGAR O. KINSMAN.
Missouri . . .	„ GEORGIANNA WOOD.	„ FRANK COLEMAN.
Arkansas . . .	„ H. VICTORIA BOYD.	„ JOHN MCPHERSON.
Michigan . . .	„ LULU THOMPSON.	„ WILLIAM LISTER.
Florida . . .	„ GEORGIE MARSTERS.	„ JAMES A. STINSON.
Texas	„ MAGGIE STINSON.	„ AMORY B. GIBBS.
Iowa	„ GEORGI'NA MEACHAM.	„ JOHN MCNAMEE.
Wisconsin . .	„ ADDIE ROWE.	„ JOSEPH COOLIDGE.
California . . .	„ DORA COLEMAN.	„ EDWARD STONE.
Minnesota . .	„ MARY G. HILLMAN.	„ CHARLES BACON.
Oregon . . .	„ AMY FERGUSON.	„ EDWARD COLEMAN.
Kansas . . .	„ CLARA FOX.	„ A. GLEASON.
West Virginia .	„ FANNY WARD.	„ CHARLES FOSTER.
Nevada . . .	„ SARAH HARRINGTON.	„ EDWARD HURD.
Nebraska . . .	„ WINNIE WALKER.	„ W. ALBERT BOYD.

The extra chorus comprised —

Miss EMELINE BECKETT.   Miss CORA TUFTS.
„ MARY A. CRAWFORD.   „ ELLA MALCOLM.
„ EVA SHERIFF.   „ CLARA A. SMITH.
„ MAY THOMAS.   „ JENNIE M. MAJOR.

Prayer, by Rev. WILLIAM WARLAND of the Episcopal Mission at East Cambridge, preceded the following programme: —

1. Hymn, "Come, Thou Almighty King" .... by the CHORUS.
   REMARKS BY REV. A. B. MUZZEY.
2. Holmes' Hymn, " Angel of Peace ; " Air, " Keller's American Hymn."
   MRS. BOWKER AND CHORUS.
   REMARKS BY REV. H. K. PERVEAR.
3. Hymn, " God bless our native land " . . . . CHORUS.
   REMARKS BY REV. C. T. JOHNSON.
4. Gilmore's Hymn, "God save our Union " . . . . . CHORUS.
   POEM BY JOHN OWEN, Esq.
5. Song, " Vive l'America!" . . . . MR. CLAUS.
   REMARKS BY JAMES ALEXANDER, Esq., of Charlotteville, Va.
9. Eichberg's Hymn, " To thee, O Country!" . . . . . CHORUS.
7. Song, "Red, White, and Blue " . . . . MRS. BOWKER.
8. Hymn, "America " . . . . CHORUS.
   REMARKS BY HIS HONOR MAYOR BRADFORD.
   POEM BY REV. WILLIAM NEWELL, D.D.
9. Song, " Star-spangled Banner " . MRS. BOWKER AND CHORUS.
   BENEDICTION BY REV. DR. NEWELL.

REMARKS OF REV. A. B. MUZZEY,

Of Cambridge.

NOTHING could be more appropriate, in the centennial celebration of Washington's taking command of the American army, than this gathering of our children. Call this what else you please, it is eminently the children's day. Washington is styled in history the Father of his Country. He had no children himself; and Providence, by not giving him any, meant evidently he should be the father of his whole country. This makes him the father of every child in the land.

But that is not all: he is specially the father of our children because he loved them; his heart went out toward all the little ones of his day. The lady he married had five of her own: to these their step-father was most warmly devoted. He delighted, for their pleasure, to gather parties under his hospitable roof; and, as he looked on their games and frolics, he became a child himself. When one of them, a beautiful daughter, lay on her death-bed, he knelt at her side in earnest prayer. It was his custom to notice children wherever he met them. In the year of his election to the Presidency he came to New England. An aged lady of my parish in Newburyport told me, that, when he rode through that town, the children, of whom she was one, were ranged in two lines; and, as he passed them, he bowed to each side, and gave them a smile she should never forget.

This is the children's day because Washington, in his own childhood and youth, was a pattern of some of the finest qualities of character. Wordsworth says, "The child is the father of the man." This was remarkably true of Washington. Every thing that the man afterwards became was foreshown in the boy. As a man he was noted for order. He found the troops on Cambridge Common without discipline, and inclined to irregularities of all sorts; but he soon brought them into order. He would allow them in no personal disputes; and, seeing once two men in a quarrel, he not only reproved them, but laid his strong arm on their shoulders and separated them. When he was made President, the government was new, and many things were at first in confusion; but he moulded them into shape, and out of chaos he brought harmony and order. Go back to the boy, and you find him systematic in all he did. At thirteen he drew up fifty-seven "Rules of Behavior." You see already in them the man. "Think before you speak." "It is good manners to prefer them to whom we speak before ourselves." "Speak not injurious words, neither in jest nor earnest." "Honor and obey your parents." "Let your recreations be manful, not sinful." "Whenever you speak of God, let it be seriously, in reverence." "Labor to keep alive in your breast that little spark of celestial fire called conscience."

As a boy, Washington made the best use of all his privileges: these were very few. One of his father's servants (named "Old Hobby") taught him his first lessons in what was called a "field-school." Afterwards he went to a common school, and poor enough it was; but the boy was noticed as "inquisitive, docile, and diligent." Reading, writing, arithmetic, and, later, book-keeping and surveying, were all he studied; but on these he built up a good education. He taught himself grammar. His early handwriting is legible, even, and handsome; and his style in composition is a model, — clear, forcible, and pure. This self-culture followed him through life.

Washington was remarkable in his manhood for bodily development, vigor, and beauty. He laid the foundation for this in his boyhood. Not stupid and sluggish, but active and alert, he was fond of sports, especially feats of bodily skill. His training prepared him for the hard campaigns of war. No soldier could endure more in camp or field than he. On to age he continued a man marked for his physical energy. Seeing two men engaged in pitching stones, said he, "I think I can beat that;" and he did beat it.

Washington began life by obedience. He had an excellent mother, left a widow when he was but four years old. She taught him well, both by precept and example. She read good books to him: we find among these Sir Matthew Hale's "Contemplations," full of wise advice. Many of its rules, read to the boy, bore good fruits in the man; made him true to himself, true to his God, true to his country. When fourteen years of age he had the offer of a midshipman's place, and was disposed to accept it. But his mother found it hard to part with him: her wishes were his law, and he gave up the plan.

This early habit of obedience fitted Washington to rise in after-life, and to fill well all the offices he held. Only by obeying do we learn to command. The two things were seen in the boy. His schoolmates used to form little companies, and George Washington was always chosen commander. Sometimes disputes would spring up between them, and he was sure to be selected as arbiter. We see in all this the germs of that wise general who could reconcile jealousies and alienations among officers on his staff and in the whole army, — germs of that grand conciliation which could keep or restore the peace in a President's cabinet made up of such conflicting elements as Jefferson, Hamilton, and Knox.

Look at the boy, and you see candor in judging others, a modest estimate of himself, economy and industry in his studies and his work as a surveyor and on the farm. From his mother he learned truthfulness, sincerity, and firmness in the right. Out of a loyal childhood came those traits, which, morally speaking, were the crown and glory of his life, — conscientiousness, an integrity on which time and temptation left no stain, and that self-sacrifice which made him a pure patriot, a brave and victorious general, an able, all-comprehending president.

I have spoken of his early schools, and of his model mother as doing so much toward educating and building up this peerless man. I wish to say, in closing, that the cornerstone of this noble edifice was laid, under God, by his own hand. Washington had a great deal to contend with in his nature. A biographer truly says, "His temperament was ardent, and his passions strong: it was his constant effort, and his ultimate triumph, to check the one, and to subdue the other."

July 3, 1775, Washington took command of the American army on this spot. For that arduous position so triumphantly sustained, and for his whole subsequent life, he prepared by *first taking command of himself.*

REMARKS OF JAMES ALEXANDER, Esq.,
Of Charlotteville, Virginia.

On being introduced by Mr. WOODWARD as coming from Virginia, the home of George Washington and Thomas Jefferson, Mr. ALEXANDER said that he felt it a great honor to be present on this occasion. This morning, in marching under the venerable elm, where, one hundred years ago, George Washington, of Virginia, unsheathed his sword, and took command of the Revolutionary army, he had reverently uncovered his head, while his heart swelled with devout adoration to the Almighty for having given to this country so pure a patriot and unselfish a man as George Washington, whom all America delights to honor as the Father of his Country. In Virginia, infant lips are taught to speak the name of Washington; and long may it continue thus to be! In Massachusetts, as in Virginia, the name of Washington is. the synonyme of all that is great, good, virtuous,. and noble. The orator of the day, as well as the eloquent poet, had rendered him and Virginia full justice.

Mr. Alexander, on turning around, said that the sight of the bright constellation of stars (young ladies representing the States in the Union) fairly bewildered him. It was a grand vision, a dazzling galaxy of light and beauty. He would, however, pay his obeisance to the fair one in that galaxy who bore across her bosom, in letters of gold, "Virginia;" and bowing to the young lady, the young lady arising, the audience gave three cheers for the State she represented.

Mr. Alexander alluded to his Virginia home, where the first thing he saw in the morning, and the last at night, was Monticello, the home and the grave of Thomas Jefferson, who penned the immortal Declaration of Independence; the wisest sage and purest patriot of any age, whose principles were destined to mould and influence governments to the most remote period of time.

Mr. Alexander here alluded to a visit of the great Massachusetts statesman, Daniel Webster, to Thomas Jefferson, and the way the Sabbath was spent by these two great men in discussing the beauties of the Bible; Mr. Webster reading, from a folio of the Scriptures of the year 1458, some of the sublime passages in Jeremiah, and Mr. Jefferson saying that the Sunday schools presented the only legitimate means, under the Constitution, of avoiding the rock on which the French republic was wrecked. Mr. Jefferson also said on that occasion, "I have always said, and always will say, that the studious perusal of the sacred volume will make better citizens, better fathers, and better husbands."

To the thousands of children before me, said Mr. Alexander, all of whom, perhaps, are Sunday-school scholars, what better advice could be given than the words of the sage of Monticello? Mr. Alexander said he had been a scholar fifty-nine years ago in Christ Church Sunday School, in the then town of Boston; and he had never forgotten the teachings of his instructors, and would cherish them to the end of life. "Remember the Sabbath-day, and keep it holy," is as binding now as it was when first promulgated from Mount Sinai. The desecration of the sabbath-day leads to all other vices, and tempts men to wickedness, and corrupts their moral nature. Daniel Webster, in his letter giving an account of his visit to Thomas Jefferson, said, "The sabbath school is one of the great institutions of the day. It leads our youth in the path of truth and morality, and makes them good men and useful citizens. As a school of religious instruction, it is of inestimable value. As a civil institution, it is priceless. It has done more to preserve our liberties than grave statesmen and armed soldiers. Let it, then, be fostered and preserved until the end of time. I once defended a man charged with the awful crime of murder. At the conclusion of the trial, I asked him what could have induced him to stain his hands with the blood of a fellow-being. Turning his blood-shot eyes full upon me, he replied, 'Mr. Webster, in my youth I spent the holy Sabbath in evil amusements, instead of frequenting the house of prayer and praise.'"

Mr. Alexander returned his thanks to the audience for the attention they had given him in his desultory remarks, saying he would carry with him to his Virginian home the recollections of this day. May God bless our common country!

UNDER THE WASHINGTON ELM.

By Rev. Wm. Newell, D.D.*

WHAT broke a hundred years ago
    The stillness of the Muses' seat?
It was no village muster's show,
    No common pageant of the street.

Seen in the sunlight of the past,
    We read its true historic worth;
Through the soft halo round it cast
    Our eyes discern a nation's birth.

Under the Massachusetts Elm
    Stood the Virginian's noble form,
Our brave, wise pilot at the helm
    In war and peace, in calm and storm.

And there, on that bright, busy day,
    From farm-house, work-shop, college, drawn,
Our patriot sires, in armed array,
    Welcomed with joy their Washington.

Chosen by God to work his will,
    His more than kingly place he found:
The work begun on Bunker Hill
    He with a glorious issue crowned.

---

* Dr. Newell was pastor of the First Parish in Cambridge from 1830 to 1868, and preached in the ancient edifice in which Washington worshipped at times during his stay in Cambridge, until the dedication of the new church built for the parish in 1833.

And the blue heavens upon him smiled;
   The angels smiled — through tears,
Seeing the bloody heaps uppiled
   Along the seven dark years.

Up from the sheath his sword!
   It flashed o'er land and sea:
With it went forth the word,
   " Our country *shall* be free!"

Under the summer sky,
   Around the towering tree,
Uprose the people's cry,
" Our country *shall* be free!"

Through the still solitudes,
   O'er meadow, field, and knoll,
Into sweet Auburn's woods
   Was borne the war-drum's roll.

Back from old Harvard's walls
   And from the house of prayer
Rang Freedom's trumpet-calls
   On the New-England air.

Echoed from town to town
   The stirring summons went;
And all hearts beat as one,
   On one great purpose bent.

Shoulder to shoulder then
   North, South, and East and West,
Stood on each battle-plain,
   Forward together pressed;

And marching, side by side,
   To one dear country bound,
Together fought and died,
   With common laurels crowned.

And what with blood they bought,
   And what they won with tears,
Blessings beyond their thought
   Fill the centennial years.

Thanks to their God and ours
    For duty nobly done!
Strew we your graves with flowers,
    Soldiers of Washington.

His honored elm still lives
    'Mid nature's wear and strife,
Shelter and shade still gives,
    Though scarred and shorn its life;

Welcomes with joy and pride
    The well-remembered day,
And, in age glorified,
    Awaits its doomed decay.

And methinks, at this feast of centennial cheer,
From its soft-rustling leaves solemn voices I hear: —

    "Glory enough," it saith:
    " Toll now my funeral-knell:
    Mine the delight in death
        This hour to see. Farewell!"

With the word of farewell, from our patriarch tree
Other words would I speak that are whispered to me:—

" What outstood the storm under Washington's hand,
And, grown in God's sunshine, o'ershadows the land,
Tree of Liberty, nourished with blood at the root,
Whose seeds scattered wide will bear more and more fruit
For the healing of nations and righting of wrong,
Oh! keep it, God's gift, root and branch, sound and strong.
Its beauty the eyes of all nations will draw
If fenced in with reason and guarded by law,
In a linked band of States, fired with national pride,
As under the old flag they march side by side.
For twin growths in our soil that no changes can sever
Stand Union and Liberty now and for ever."

And under the sacred memorial tree,
With prayers for the nation that is and to be,
Here and now, young and old, oh! let us renew
The patriot's vows to the Red, White, and Blue;
To the flag that we hold the more dear for its scars,
With its stars shining bright, and the *whole* of its stars."

Hear, O God! thy children's prayer,
As on this glad day we swear
To our country to be true
In what we say and what we do;
And, when the word our country gives,
Offer our fortunes and our lives.

God, our Father, hear us now,
And record the solemn vow.

Hear, O God! thy children's prayer,
As on this glad day we swear
Blood-bought Freedom to maintain
With the blessings in its train;
Giving equal rights to all,
White or black, in hut or hall.

God, our Father, hear us now,
And record the solemn vow.

Hear, O God! thy children's prayer,
As on this glad day we swear
Our great Union to uphold
Now, as in the days of old:
North and South, and East and West,
In each other's blessings blest.

God, our Father, hear us now,
And record the solemn vow.

All that makes us strong and great,
Freedom's fruits in Church and State,
Help us in thy fear to hold,
And to nobler issues mould.
But from passion, sin, and strife,
If the Saviour set us free,
Ours is then the heavenward life,
Ours the sweetest liberty.

After the benediction, Mr. WOODWARD announced that a good friend of the children had provided for them five hundred pounds, making two thousand packages, of candy. The generous donor had declined to allow his name to be announced, but had yielded to a request to allow the experiment of spelling it with a " magic wand." The experiment being tried, and the necessary catch-words ingeniously put by Mr. WOODWARD, many of the children quickly discovered the name to be " SAMUEL B. RINDGE ; " after which the packages were distributed, and the enthusiastic children closed their entertainment with tumultuous cheers.

THE EVENING CONCERT.

At sunset, a national salute of thirty-seven guns was fired by Battery A.

From six to eight o'clock, the bells on Christ Church were chimed by Mr. Henry P. Munroe.

At eight o'clock, a concert was given on the Common by Edmands' Military Band, Thomas O. Edmands *leader;* and the following chorus, under direction of Augustus W. Fix: —

First Tenor.	Second Tenor.
Daniel C. McCallar.	Charles H. Danforth.
James F. Bird.	Edward Davies.
Ezra H. Stevens.	Charles J. Wood.
George J. Bird.	John W. Wood.
Jacob B. Shaw.	William A. Hunnewell.
Charles Grieves.	Roger S. Rundlett.
William R. Bateman.	

First Bass.	Second Bass.
B. Otis Danforth.	John F. Ward.
Herbert E. Valentine.	John S. Sawyer.
Henry Stevens.	Charles Bates.
Albert J. Sawyer.	Benjamin L. Ward.
Carlos Nudd.	Francis L. Pratt.

PROGRAMME.

1. National Airs . . . . . .
   Band.
2. American Hymn . . . . . . *Keller.*
   Chorus.

3. Overture Brillante, "Vallei des Roses" . . . . . . *Rolle.*
　　　　BAND.
4. Praise of the Soldier . . . . *Boieldieu.*
　　　　CHORUS.
5. Waltzes, "Tausend und eine Nachts" . . . . *Strauss.*
　　　　BAND.
6. "How have I loved thee, Native Land!" . . . . . *Mohring.*
　　　　CHORUS.
7. Quickstep, "Silver Threads among the Gold" . . . *Downing.*
　　　　BAND.
8. *a.* "How can I leave Thee?" . . . . *Cramer.*
   b. Drinking Song . . . . *Mohring.*
　　　　CHORUS.
9. Polka for Cornet . . . . *Selected.*
　　　　SOLO BY MR. D. W. BOARDMAN.
10. Oh! Shout, Men of Strength . . . . *Tenney.*
　　　　CHORUS.
11. Centennial Hymn . . . . *Converse.*
　　　　BAND.
12. "To thee, O Country!" . . . . *Eichberg.*
　　　　CHORUS.
13. Selections from "La Fille de Madame Angot" . . *Lecocq.*
　　　　BAND.
14. Artillerists' Oath . . . . *Adams.*
　　　　CHORUS.
15. Waltzes "Girofle Girofla" . . . . *Lecocq.*
　　　　BAND.
16. *a.* "He who is Upright" . . . . *Flemming.*
    b. "Bright Sword of Liberty" . . . . *Weber.*
　　　　CHORUS.
17. Serenade . . . . *Boulcourd.*
　　　　BAND.
18. The Gay Pilgrim . . . . *Mangold.*
　　　　CHORUS.
19. Concert Medley . . . . *Selected.*
　　　　BAND.
20. The Watch on the Rhine . . . . *Wilheld.*
　　　　CHORUS.
21. 1. Galop, "Reito" . . . . *Piefke.*
    2. Sweet Home . . . . *Payne.*
　　　　BAND.

From eight thousand to ten thousand persons were estimated to have been present on the Common during the evening, besides large numbers in carriages parked in the surrounding streets.

Two thousand Chinese-lanterns adorned the various paths, the monument, and the ancient elm; and the whole scene was enlivened and made effective by brilliant-colored fires, which were burned without intermission till eleven o'clock, filling the place with a dazzling radiance. Upon the top of the Union-Railway office was placed a powerful calcium-light, which gave a magnificent effect to the decorations in Harvard Square and to the college-buildings.

It is worthy of notice, that there was no accident to cast a shadow upon the festivities of the day.

SOLDIERS' MONUMENT, CAMBRIDGE.

GOVERNMENT
OF
THE CITY OF CAMBRIDGE,
1875.

MAYOR.
HON. ISAAC BRADFORD.

ALDERMEN.

WALTER S. BLANCHARD, GEORGE H. HOWARD,
BENJAMIN F. DAVIES, JOHN H. LEIGHTON,
RUSSELL S. EDWARDS, SAMUEL L. MONTAGUE,
LEANDER GREELY, JONAS C. WELLINGTON,
LEANDER M. HANNUM, WILLIAM L. WHITNEY.

ALDERMEN BY WARDS. — Ward I. Alderman Whitney. Ward II. Aldermen Blanchard and Montague. Ward III. Aldermen Davies, Howard, and Leighton. Ward IV. Aldermen Greely and Hannum. Ward V. Aldermen Edwards and Wellington.

Clerk. — Justin A. Jacobs.

COMMON COUNCIL.
GEORGE F. PIPER, *President.*

WARD I. — Lemuel Kempton, Charles Moore, John T. G. Nichols, Walter S. Swan.

WARD II. — Henry D. Forbes, Thomas A. Graham, David Heffernan, James Mellen, Jr., Hibbard P. Ross.

WARD III. — John Clary, William E. Doyle, Alexander Fraser, Joseph J. Kelly, Charles Quinn.

WARD IV. — Frank A. Allen, Edmund Reardon, Sulvilyer H. Sanborn, John Stone.

WARD V. — Jeremiah Murphy, George F. Piper.

Clerk: Jos. Warren Cotton.   *Page:* Allan P. Kelly.

City Clerk. — Justin A. Jacobs.
Clerk of Committees. — Jos. Warren Cotton.
City Solicitor. — John W. Hammond.
City Engineer. — Josiah G. Chase.
Superintendent of Streets. — George L. Cade.
Superintendent of Lamps. — John Cahill.
Commissioner on W. Boston and Craigie's Bridges. — Ezra Parmenter.
City Messenger: Francis L. Pratt. *Ass't Messenger:* Charles A. Gay.

FINANCIAL DEPARTMENT.

Auditor of Accounts. — Justin A. Jacobs.
Treasurer. — Joseph Whitney.
Assessors. — Levi L. Cushing, Jr., Artemas Z. Brown, Andrew J. Green.
Assistant Assessors — Thomas Stearns, Samuel Sanders, Bernard J. McCormic, Benjamin F. Nourse, James H. Cutter.
Commissioners on Sinking Funds of the City. — The Mayor, City Treasurer, Alderman Whitney, and the President of the Common Council, *ex officio ;* Lewis Hall, Hamlin R. Harding, John M. Tyler.
Trustees of Sinking Fund of Water Loan. — The Mayor, City Treasurer, and the President of the Common Council.

COMMITTEES OF THE CITY COUNCIL.

JOINT STANDING COMMITTEES.

ON FINANCE. — The Mayor. *Aldermen:* William L. Whitney, Samuel L. Montague. *Common Council:* The President, Edmund Reardon, James Mellen, Jr., Joseph J. Kelly, Walter S. Swan, Frank A. Allen.

ON PUBLIC INSTRUCTION. — *Aldermen:* Benjamin F. Davies, Leander M. Hannum. *Common Council:* The President, Joseph J. Kelly, Henry D. Forbes, Walter S. Swan.

ON ORDINANCES. — *Aldermen:* Walter S. Blanchard, Leander Greely. *Common Council:* John T. G. Nichols, John Stone, Henry D. Forbes.

ON ACCOUNTS. — *Aldermen:* Russell S. Edwards, George H. Howard. *Common Council:* John Clary, Frank A. Allen, John T. G. Nichols.

ON PUBLIC PROPERTY. — *Aldermen:* Leander M. Hannum, Samuel L. Montague. *Common Council:* John Clary, Lemuel Kempton, Jeremiah Murphy.

ON THE ALMSHOUSE. — *Aldermen:* Samuel L. Montague, Jonas C. Wellington. *Common Council:* Alexander Fraser, William E. Doyle, David Heffernan.

ON ROADS AND BRIDGES. — *Aldermen:* William L. Whitney, Walter S. Blanchard. *Common Council:* Edmund Reardon, Thomas A. Graham, Charles Quinn.

ON FUEL. — *Aldermen:* Benjamin F. Davies, Samuel L. Montague. *Common Council:* Alexander Fraser, Charles Moore, David Heffernan.

ON LAMPS. — *Aldermen:* Leander M. Hannum, Russell S. Edwards. *Common Council:* Charles Quinn, Hibbard P. Ross, Charles Moore.

ON WATERING STREETS. — *Aldermen:* George H. Howard, Leander Greely. *Common Council:* James Mellen, Jr., Lemuel Kempton, Jeremiah Murphy.

ON PRINTING. — *Alderman:* William L. Whitney. *Common Council:* John Stone, Sulvilyer H. Sanborn.

ON THE FIRE DEPARTMENT. — *Aldermen:* George H. Howard, Leander Greely. *Common Council:* Sulvilyer H. Sanborn, Thomas A. Graham, Lemuel Kempton.

THE CITY GOVERNMENT.

ON CITY ENGINEERING. — *Aldermen:* Walter S. Blanchard, Russell S. Edwards. *Common Council:* Hibbard P. Ross, Joseph J. Kelly, William E. Doyle.

ON ASSESSORS' DEPARTMENT. — *Alderman:* John H. Leighton. *Common Council:* Charles Moore, Hibbard P. Ross.

JOINT SPECIAL COMMITTEE.

ON SOLDIERS AND THEIR FAMILIES. — *Aldermen:* Jonas C. Wellington, John H. Leighton. *Common Council:* John T. G. Nichols, James Mellen, Jr., William E. Doyle, John Stone, Jeremiah Murphy.

STANDING COMMITTEES OF THE BOARD OF MAYOR AND ALDERMEN.

ON POLICE. — The Mayor, William L. Whitney, Samuel L. Montague, John H. Leighton.

ON THE FIRE DEPARTMENT. — George H. Howard, Leander Greely, Jonas C. Wellington.

ON ROADS AND BRIDGES. — William L. Whitney, Walter S. Blanchard, Benjamin F. Davies.

ON SEWERS AND DRAINS. — Leander Greely, Jonas C. Wellington, John H. Leighton.

ON LICENSES. — Russell S. Edwards, Leander M. Hannum, George H. Howard.

ON HEALTH. — John H. Leighton, William L. Whitney, Walter S. Blanchard.

STANDING COMMITTEES OF THE COMMON COUNCIL.

ON ELECTIONS AND RETURNS. — Alexander Fraser, Edmund Reardon, Thomas A. Graham.

ON BILLS IN THE SECOND READING. — John Clary, Frank A. Allen, David Heffernan.

ON ENROLLED ORDINANCES. — Sulvilyer H. Sanborn, Henry D. Forbes, Walter S. Swan.

BOARD OF HEALTH.

The Mayor and Aldermen.

SURVEYORS OF HIGHWAYS.

The same persons who compose the Board of Mayor and Aldermen.

SCHOOL COMMITTEE.

ISAAC BRADFORD, Mayor, *ex officio, Chairman.*

WARD I. — Andrew P. Peabody, Edwin B. Hale, John L. Hildreth.
    ,, II. — William S. Karr, Edward R. Cogswell, Henry Hinckley.
    ,, III. — Samuel W. McDaniel, John O'Brien, Albert L. Norris.
    ,, IV. — George E. McNeil, James A. Dow, George R. Leavitt.
    ,, V. — Wm. S. Apsey, Philip R. Ammidon, Theop. G. Wadman.

Secretary: W. W. Wellington. *Superintendent of Schools:* Francis Cogswell.

N.B. — For list of teachers in the public schools, see p. 124.

OVERSEERS OF THE POOR.

The Mayor, *ex officio, Chairman. One Year:* Benjamin F. Wyeth, George D. Chamberlain, Jeremiah H. Mulcahy. *Two Years:* Sylvanus M. Parsons, Joseph Newmarch, Lewis B. Guyer.
Clerk. — Benjamin F. Wyeth.
Warden of the Almshouse. — Joseph W. Averill.
Physician of the Almshouse. — James R. Morse, M.D.

REPRESENTATIVES IN GENERAL COURT.

Levi L. Cushing, Jr., Daniel H. Thurston, Edward Kendall, Austin C. Wellington, Jeremiah W. Coveney.

POLICE COURT.

Standing Justice: John S. Ladd. *Special Justices:* Henry W. Muzzey, Woodward Emery. *Clerk:* Thomas McIntire.

WATER DEPARTMENT.

Cambridge Water Board. — The Mayor, and President of the Common Council, *ex officio.* J. Warren Merrill, Chester W. Kingsley (President), Henry L. Eustis, George P. Carter, Samuel Slocomb.
Clerk. — Justin A. Jacobs.
Superintendent of Waterworks. — Samuel W. Dudley.
Water Registrar. — Abiel F. Fifield.

CAMBRIDGE CEMETERY.

Commissioners. — The Mayor, *ex officio.* George T. Gale, William Page, George S. Saunders, Curtis Davis, George R. Brine, John M. Tyler.
Superintendent. — James K. Farwell.

TRUSTEES OF DANA LIBRARY.

The Mayor, *ex officio, Chairman. Alderman:* William L. Whitney. *Common Council:* George F. Piper. *Citizens at Large:* John S. March, Charles Deane, John B. Taylor. *Librarian:* Miss Almira L. Hayward. *Secretary:* John S. March.

TRUSTEES OF THE DOWSE INSTITUTE.

The Mayor, and President of the Common Council, *ex officio.* John C. Dodge, William W. Wellington, Willard A. Bullard.

TRUSTEES OF THE SANDERS TEMPERANCE FUND.

The Mayor, and President of the Common Council, *ex officio. Alderman:* Jonas C. Wellington. *Common Council:* John Clary, John Stone.

THE CITY GOVERNMENT. 121

FIRE DEPARTMENT.

BOARD OF ENGINEERS. — *Chief Engineer:* Patrick H. Raymond. *Assistant Engineers:* First Assistant, Thomas J. Casey; Second Assistant, Richard F. Tobin; Third Assistant, Daniel O'Connell; Fourth Assistant, John P. Farmer, Jr. *Clerk of the Board:* John P. Farmer, Jr.
Steam Fire-Engine Company, No. One, Foreman, William H. Emory; *No. Two,* William B. Cade; *No. Three,* William Parker; *No. Four,* Benjamin Young; *No. Five,* Francis P. Scanlan. *Hook-and-Ladder Company, No. One,* Foreman, James P. Ewell; *No. Two,* James Dalton. *Supply Hose, No. One,* Driver, Lewis C. Clark.

POLICE DEPARTMENT.

Chief of Police. — George H. Copeland.
Captains of Police. — *District I.* Timothy Ames. *District II.* William Twist. *District III.* John L. Boynton.
Captain of Night Police. — Frederick W. Hagar.
Policemen. — *District I.* Thomas D. Cook, James B. Morse, Micah W. Cook, Andrew Sproul, Andrew G. Smith, George A. Marston, Benjamin Kennard, L. J. Cloyes, William T. Gibson, James Miller, Leonard Shackford, Daniel Callahan, William H. Fitzpatrick, John Le Barron, Frederic B. Pullen, Albert D. Cleveland, Henry M. Tyler, Alonzo S. Harriman, Thomas W. Penney, William Evans, Jr., Hugh McNamee. *District II.* Benjamin F. Bridden, Daniel Sherman, James H. Parks, George Wood, Warner W. Simonds, John Coleman, Calvin C. Smith, Luther Hapgood, Simon D. Hiscock, Rufus S. Downe, George Cox, Charles B. Jones, James E. Murray, John Little, Thomas S. Hall, Charles W. Rugg, William Nickelson, Lawrence Ducy, Michael A. Dalton, James Daily, James S. Alexander. *District III.* William Mullett, Dennis Corcoran, Moses W. Hooper, John F. Murray, Matthew R. Moore, Amos Jones, David N. McCleary, Stephen E. Day, John Collier, Warren A. Eaton, Otis Dennison, John W. Skelley, John Jackson.
Keeper of Lock-ups. — George H. Copeland.
Truant-Officers. — Mark J. Folsom, Moses M. Child, George S. Dudley, Augustus P. Griffing, Francis M. Mason.
Constables. — George H. Copeland, William Twist, John L. Boynton, John C. Burdakin, Thomas Work, Thomas McIntire, Charles H. Hunnewell, Charles J. Adams, James F. Jefferds, John W. Skelley, Warner W. Simonds, Thomas D. Cook, Charles L. Russell, Benjamin King, Patrick H. Raymond, Thomas T. Ferguson, Timothy Ames, John Cahill, M. S. Busnach, William Dickson, Edward S. English, W. A. Taylor, Amos Jones, George F. McKenzie, E. B. Ramsdell, Michael A. Keenan, Reuben A. Adams, George L. Mitchell, Calvin Ford.
Special Policemen. — P. H. Raymond, Thomas J. Casey, Joseph H. Marvin, Samuel W. Dudley, Daniel O'Connell, John P. Farmer, Jr.,

Thomas H. Eames, Edward F. Belcher, Roland Litchfield, Charles L.
Russell, William L. Locklin, G. C. W. Fuller, J. L. P. Ackers, Charles
H. Wiggin, B. A. Brown, Lucius A. Buck, James F. Jefferds, Joseph W.
Averill, Roland Litchfield, Jr., James C. Wilder, Thomas McIntire, James
K. Farwell, Hiram Nevons, James M. Learned, George Henderson,
George Dale, Jesse H. Kittredge, George Smith, Charles P. Allen, Samuel F. Hunt, George J. Sutton, Joseph Bebo, Alexis Brusseau, Anthony
Chalifrau, Patrick Dunnigan, Moore R. Homer, Thomas Cowen, Noah
M. Cofran, Benjamin F. Livingston, Charles A. Gay, James W. Lovering, George B. Lothrop, Orlando B. Richardson, Richard F. Tobin,
Charles H. Winslow, Joseph Collins, E. G. Hall, George T. Barrington,
Michael Ginty, John L. Sproul, Joseph Smith, William Kelly, E. F.
Young, George Putnam, Thomas Briney, George S. Pike, William H.
Grieves, A. A. Barker, G. E. S. Hutchins, William Martin, F. W.
Blumve, Joseph G. Glazier, Joseph Moran, Joshua S. Sanborn, George
W. Wright, George W. Metcalf, George T. R. Roberts, George Stott,
Charles A. True, Joseph K. Tarbox, John McGrath, Walter E. Mellish,
Joseph Baker, Thomas Langlan, Jacob Foster, Thomas J. Saunders,
John Mahady, Alexander F. Shepherd, Edward E. Farrar, William Hunnewell, Daniel R. Melcher, John Hughes, Frank Goudraw, Frederick H.
Greenwood, Frank J. Curtis, George H. Sherman, George E. Goodwin,
Francis M. Mason, Mark J. Folsom, Moses M. Child, George S. Dudley,
Augustus P. Griffing, William Porter, Charles H. Stetson, John Axtman.

Superintendent of Burial Ground, Ward I. — Benjamin F. Wyeth.

Undertakers. — Benjamin F. Wyeth, Roland Litchfield, Samuel F.
Hunt, Thomas Devens, John W. Coveney, Judson Litchfield, William
Casey, C. Henry Lockhart, Alvah A. Hadley, Benjamin J. Hoyt, W. A.
Taylor, William C. Walker.

Auctioneers. — Samuel R. Knights, G. C. W. Fuller, Oliver R. Osborn,
Humphrey L. Snow, Samuel F. Rugg, Thomas T. Ferguson, C. F. Boynton, John C. Farnham, John L. Porter, Edward Burnham, George C.
Hosmer, George O. Knox, Henry A. Burkett, Benjamin King, Michael
James Moss, Orrin P. Kinne, John R. Fairbairn, Edward H. Carter,
George F. McKenzie, Samuel C. Knights, Jeremiah W. Coveney, James
C. Wilder, John Cahill, T. W. Ray, Reuben A. Adams, Edwin P. Henderson.

Fence-Viewers. — George B. Lothrop, Abiel Goss, Abel Stevens.

Field-Drivers. — The several policemen of Districts I., II., and III.

Measurers of Wood and Bark. — John R. Taylor, Francis H. White,
Benjamin J. Hoyt, J. Henry Wyman, John F. Brine.

Pound-Keepers. — James Gilligan, Thomas D. Cook, George A. Marston.

Fish-Officers. — Thomas D. Cook, Joseph W. Averill, Andrew Sproul.

Hay-Weighers. — Timothy Sullivan, William C. Brooks, William H.
Dodge, Francis H. White, John F. Brine, Harrison G. Woodward.

THE CITY GOVERNMENT. 123

Coal-Weighers. — James F. Jefferds, John F. Brine, Thomas McIntire. William A. Hunnewell, J. Henry Wyman, William C. Brooks, Jones Valentine, Alfred H. Wellington, Harrison G. Woodward, Malachi Mullen.

Weigher of Boilers and Heavy Machinery. — Harrison G. Woodward.

Weighers. — Joseph W. Averill, Patrick Dunnigan, Edmund Reardon, James H. Reardon, Henry Hooker, Thomas Ralph, George W. Wright, Joshua S. Sanborn.

Sealer of Weights and Measures, Inspector of Milk, Inspector of Charcoal Baskets, and Measurer of Grain. — John Cahill.

Surveyors of Mechanics' Work. — William S. Barbour, William A. Mason, John S. Pollard.

Measurer and Surveyor. — E. F. Young.

Inspectors of Junk-Shops. — George H. Copeland, Amos Jones, Warner W. Simonds.

WARD OFFICERS.

WARD I. — *Warden:* Henry R. Glover. *Clerk:* Francis L. Pratt. *Inspectors:* Joseph Williams, Edmund Miles, Nathaniel Munroe.

WARD II. — *Warden:* Charles F. Thurston. *Clerk:* Harry B. Winnett. *Inspectors:* Walter H. Harding, Charles E. Pierce, George A. Leonard.

WARD III. — *Warden:* Luther L. Parker. *Clerk:* Andrew Fogg. *Inspectors:* Augustus W. Fix, Daniel Shaughnessy, James J. Colman.

WARD IV. — *Warden:* Charles L. Russell. *Clerk:* Benjamin F. Hastings. *Inspectors:* James F. White, William H. Ackers, Zephaniah H. Thomas, Jr.

WARD V. — *Warden:* Francis M. Mason. *Clerk:* Francis H. White. *Inspectors:* Charles L. Fuller, Henry K. Parsons, Charles F. Fay.

TEACHERS IN THE PUBLIC SCHOOLS.

HIGH SCHOOL.— Lyman R. Williston, William F. Bradbury, Theodore P. Adams, John Orne, Jr., Solon F. Whitney, Mary F. Peirce. Augusta L. Brigham, Olive E. Fairbanks, Hannah Gleason, Emma A. Scudder, Mary C. C. Goddard, Emma F. Munroe.
GRAMMAR SCHOOLS. — *Allston:* Benjamin W. Roberts, Lizzie B. Winnett, Emma F. King, Emily R. Pitkin, Sarah G. Hinkley, Hannah L. Hill, Minnie L. McKay, Hattie E. Keith, Emma E. Perkins, Susan H. Ricker, Ida G. Smith, Lucia E. Whiting, Etta Woods. *Harvard:* Aaron B. Magoun, Augusta H. Dodge, Ada H. Wellington, Margaret B. Wellington, Mary E. Wyeth, Susan F. Athearn, Emily F. Damon, Sarah E. Dyer, Mary F. Emerson, Sarah E. Golden, Margaret R. Hodgkins, Sarah E. Hearsey, Lydia S. King, Annie M. Leland, Susan E. Merrill, Ellen Merrick. *Putnam:* James S. Barrell, Sarah M. Burnham, Ella R. Grieves, Eliza M. Hussey, Charlotte A. Brown, Augusta G. Mirick, Sarah L. Merrill, Addie Stone, Marion H. Burnham, Carrie Close. *Shepard:* Daniel B. Wheeler, Mary C. Cooke, Emma M. Taylor, Estelle H. Varney, John Wilson, Sara J. French, S. F. Gordon, Harriet L. Hayward, Julia H. Osgood, Sarah A. Rand, Cora M. Wheeler. *Thorndike:* Ruel H. Fletcher, Ellen M. Parker, Martha A. Martin, Mary E. Nason, Isabella B. Tenney, Fannie Allen, Ella W. Clark, Ruth H. Faxon, Emma A. Hopkins, Abby A. K. Howard, Mary A. Willis, Grace W. Fletcher. *Washington:* Daniel Mansfield, Hattie T. Nealley, Lucy A. Downing, Adeline M. Ireson, Emma F. Veazie, Adelia Dunham, Ada E. Doe, Abbie' J. Hodgkins, Adelaide A. Keeler, Dora Puffer, Abby M. Webb, Abbie M. Holder. *Webster:* John D. Billings, Gertrude B. Hale, Charlotte M. Chase, Louise C. D. Harlow, Mary E. Towle, Gertrude A. Hyde, Esther F. Hannum, Susan B. Holmes, Carrie M. Kingman, Anna S. Lamson, Hattie E. Warfield, Clara E. Matchett, Emily H. Phinney, Alice Gray.
PRIMARY SCHOOLS. — *Boardman:* Adah W. Baker, Augusta L. Balch, Fannie A. Cooke, S. N. Chamberlain, Eliza A. Dow, Mary A. Lewis, Sarah E. Stewart, Nettie Sargent. *Bridge:* Elizabeth E. Dallinger, Emily C. Dallinger. *City:* Etta S. Adams, Nellie A. Hutchins. *Dana:* Abby A. Lewis, Maria F. Williams. *Dunster:* M. Louise Akerman,

Mary E. Smallidge, Sarah B. Waitt, Susan E. Wyeth. *Felton:* Georgianna L. Backus, Lizzie C. Capen, Sarah L. Cutler, Eliza J. Cutler, A. M. Houghton, Ella L. Lynes. *Gannett:* Sarah J. A. Davis, Estelle J. French, Anna M. Jones, Lottie E. Mitchell, Lucy C. Wyeth. *Gore:* Harriet A. Butler, Addie M. Bettinson, Mary A. Bourne, Agnes M. Cox, Mary E. Hartwell, Jennie A. Norris, Frances E. Pendexter, Alice J. Winward. *Harvard:* Ellen A. Cheney, Helen M. Ward, Florence M. Hayward. *Holmes:* Mary L. Bullard, Eunice W. Field, Louisa G. Matchett, Marianne M. Webb. *Mason:* M. Lizzie Evans, Alma A. Smith. *Otis:* Martha H. Butler, Luvia Goodnow, Annie Knapp, Ellen N. Pike, Carrie H. Smith, Abby S. Taylor, Lydia A. Whitcher, Kate F. Wellington. *Putnam:* Nellie F. Ball. *Quincy:* T. G. Abercrombie, Charlotte E. Jewell, Nellie Johnson. *Reed:* Harriet N. Keyes, Lucy T. Sawyer, Evelyn A. Sawyer, Elizabeth A. Tower. *Sargent:* Mary A. Brown, M. E. Dickson, Annie M. Harrod, Frances J. Harrod. *Willard:* Evelina Brooks, Fannie E. Cooke, Susan M. Cochran, H. Flora Hannum, Kate M. Lowell, Mary E. Sawyer, Mary Ann Tarbell, Amelia Wright, Laura Wright, Grace R. Woodward. *Wyman:* Fannie E. M. Dennis, Letitia M. Dennis, M. Carrie Dickman, Charlotte A. Ewell. *Training School:* Anna C. Sullivan, M. Etta Arkerson, Emma B. Alley, Jenny Prescott, Ella C. Whitney.

Teacher of Singing. — Nathan Lincoln.
Superintendent of Schools. — Francis Cogswell.

CITY OF CAMBRIDGE.

CHRONOLOGICAL CATALOGUE

FROM

THE ORGANIZATION OF THE CITY GOVERNMENT,

IN 1846, TO 1875.

	MAYOR.	CITY CLERK.	PRESIDENT OF THE COMMON COUNCIL.	CLERK OF THE COMMON COUNCIL.	TREASURER.
1846.	James D. Green.	Lucius R. Paige.	Isaac Livermore.	Charles S. Newell.	Abel W. Bruce.
1847.	James D. Green.	Lucius R. Paige.	John Sargent.	Charles S. Newell.	Abel W. Bruce.
1848.	Sidney Willard.	Lucius R. Paige.	John C. Dodge.	Charles S. Newell.	Abel W. Bruce.
1849.	Sidney Willard.	Lucius R. Paige.	Samuel P. Heywood.	Eben M. Dunbar.	Samuel Slocomb.
1850.	Sidney Willard.	Lucius R. Paige.	Samuel P. Heywood.	Eben M. Dunbar.	Samuel Slocomb.
1851.	George Stevens.	Lucius R. Paige.	John S. Ladd.	Eben M. Dunbar.	Samuel Slocomb.
1852.	George Stevens.	Lucius R. Paige.	John Sargent.	Eben M. Dunbar.	Samuel Slocomb.
1853.	James D. Green.	Lucius R. Paige.	John Sargent.	Eben M. Dunbar.	Samuel Slocomb.
1854.	Abraham Edwards.	Lucius R. Paige.	John C. Dodge.	Henry Thayer.	Samuel Slocomb.
1855.	Zebina L. Raymond.	Lucius R. Paige.	Alanson Bigelow.	Henry Thayer.	A. J. Webber.
1856.	John Sargent.	Henry Thayer.	George S. Saunders.	James M. Chase.	Joseph A. Holmes.
1857.	John Sargent.	Justin A. Jacobs.	George S. Saunders.	James M. Chase.	Joseph A. Holmes.
1858.	John Sargent.	Justin A. Jacobs.	James C. Fisk.	James M. Chase.	Joseph Whitney.
1859.	John Sargent.	Justin A. Jacobs.	James C. Fisk.	James M. Chase.	Joseph Whitney.
1860.	James D. Green.	Justin A. Jacobs.	Hamlin R. Harding.	James M. Chase.	Joseph Whitney.
1861.	James D. Green.	Justin A. Jacobs.	Hamlin R. Harding.	James M. Chase.	Joseph Whitney.
1862.	Charles Theo. Russell.	Justin A. Jacobs.	Jared Shepard.	Joseph G. Holt.	Joseph Whitney.
1863.	George C. Richardson.	Justin A. Jacobs.	George S. Saunders.	Joseph G. Holt.	Joseph Whitney.
1864.	Zebina L. Raymond.	Justin A. Jacobs.	George S. Saunders.	Joseph G. Holt.	Joseph Whitney.
1865.	J. Warren Merrill.	Justin A. Jacobs.	John S. March.	Joseph G. Holt.	Joseph Whitney.
1866.	J. Warren Merrill.	Justin A. Jacobs.	John S. March.	Joseph G. Holt.	Joseph Whitney.
1867.	Ezra Parmenter.	Justin A. Jacobs.	Marshall T. Bigelow.	Joseph G. Holt.	Joseph Whitney.
1868.	Charles H. Saunders.	Justin A. Jacobs.	Henry W. Muzzey.	J. Warren Cotton.	Joseph Whitney.
1869.	Charles H. Saunders.	Justin A. Jacobs.	Henry W. Muzzey.	J. Warren Cotton.	Joseph Whitney.
1870.	Hamlin R. Harding.	Justin A. Jacobs.	Joseph H. Converse.	J. Warren Cotton.	Joseph Whitney.
1871.	Hamlin R. Harding.	Justin A. Jacobs.	Joseph H. Converse.	J. Warren Cotton.	Joseph Whitney.
1872.	Henry O. Houghton.	Justin A. Jacobs.	Alvaro Blodgett.	J. Warren Cotton.	Joseph Whitney.
1873.	Isaac Bradford.	Justin A. Jacobs.	Alvaro Blodgett.	J. Warren Cotton.	Joseph Whitney.
1874.	Isaac Bradford.	Justin A. Jacobs.	George F. Piper.	J. Warren Cotton.	Joseph Whitney.
1875.	Isaac Bradford.	Justin A. Jacobs.	George F. Piper.	J. Warren Cotton.	Joseph Whitney.

CITY OF CAMBRIDGE.

POLLS, VALUATION, AND TAXES.

1846.

POLLS, 3224.   INHABITANTS, 12,500.

Valuation of Real Estate	$6,378,836.00
Valuation of Personal Estate	2,933,645.00
Total Valuation	$9,312,481.00
Rate of Taxation	$5 on $1000
City Tax for 1846	$44,000

1856.

POLLS, 4806.   INHABITANTS, 20,473.

Valuation of Real Estate	$12,467,950.00
Valuation of Personal Estate	5,570,700.00
Total Valuation	$18,038,650.00
Rate of Taxation	$7.70 on $1000
City Tax for 1856	$125,790.88

1866.

POLLS, 7253.   DWELLINGS, 4591.   INHABITANTS, 29,114.

Valuation of Real Estate	$17,803,400.00
Valuation of Personal Estate	10,582,300.00
Total Valuation	$28,385,700.00
Rate of Taxation	$13.20 on $1000
City Tax for 1866	$293,562.40

1875.

POLLS, 11,983.   DWELLINGS, 7676.   INHABITANTS, 47,838.

Valuation of Real Estate	$50,155,300.00
Valuation of Personal Estate	16,467,715.25
Total Valuation	$66,623,015.25
Rate of Taxation	$17 on $1000
City Tax for 1875	$1,011,000

www.ingramcontent.com/pod-product-compliance
Lightning Source LLC
Chambersburg PA
CBHW022136160426
43197CB00009B/1305